Claus Hessler's
Camp Duty Update

Snare Drum Rudiments: Bridging the Gap Between Past and Present

- **History** of European and American Drumming Traditions
- Traditional Pieces taken from the **U.S. Camp & Garrison Duty**
- A Guideline for the **Interpretation of Rudiments**
- **Modern Versions** of Rudimental Classics, Quicksteps, and **Play-Alongs**

Includes Traditional and Modern Drum Pieces & Play-Alongs

MW00826317

Alfred Music
LEARN · TEACH · PLAY

© 2017 by **Alfred** Music Publishing GmbH
alfred.com
alfredmusic.de | alfredUK.com
All Rights Reserved
Printed in Germany
item-#: 00-20255US (Book & MP3 CD)
ISBN-10: 3-943638-19-7
ISBN-13: 978-3-943638-19-6

Cover Design: Thomas Petzold
Cover Photo: Claus Hessler
Backcover Photo: Florian Alexandru-Zorn
Engraving & Layout: Claus Hessler
CD-Recording: Claus Hessler
English Translation: Anthony Copnall
Editing: Thomas Petzold & Raj Mallikarjuna
Head of Production: Thomas Petzold

Acknowledgements

My thanks to:

- my family, for constantly accepting my addiction to drumming.

- Mattl Dörsam for the fife recording.

- Alfred Music Publishing (Thomas Petzold and Helge Kuhnert) for their great work and assistance.

- my students, for being the human guinea pigs and beta testers for my educational projects.

- Patrice Schneider for additional help with editing.

- Jochen Hock for sound and mixing.

- Anthony Copnall for helping with the English translation.

- other *rudiment-addicted* drummates, in alphabetical order:

Alex Acuña	John C. Moon
Wolfgang Basler	Rainer Römer
Ed Boyle	Werner Schmitt
Robert Brenner	Steve Smith
Dom Famularo	Jochen Sponsel
Vic Firth	Greg Tunesi
David Garibaldi	Stefan Wandel
Matt Halpern	John Wooton
Ralph Hardimon	

- the companies/endorsement partners that support me and my work:

  Musik & Technik, Marburg: Michael Lange, Frank Rohe, Gerd Lücking
  Mapex Drums: Joe Hibbs, Otto Choi
  Cooperman Rope Tension Drums: Patsy and Jim Ellis
  Sabian Cymbals: Christian Koch, Nadine Metayer
  Promark Drumsticks: Kyle Thomas, Elijah Navarro
  Evans Drumheads: Marco Soccoli, Steve Lobmaier, Jim Bailey, Stephan Hänisch, and Marcus Lipperer
  Gon Bops Percussion
  The Drummer Shoe: Tom Beck

*This book is dedicated to the memory of **Vic Firth** and **Joe Hibbs**. Sadly, they both passed away before the English version of this book was completed. Both were unique in their love and passion for drumming, and truly believed in supporting music education.*

About the Author

In the drum world, Claus Hessler is not only well known as an institution of the Moeller Technique, but has also set standards in drum education with his international publications *Open Handed Playing, Volumes 1 and 2, Daily Drumset Workout,* and his double DVD *Drumming Kairos.*

Because Claus works as an international clinician, you might meet him at drum events anywhere from Mexico to Australia. As an author, he regularly writes for drum magazines such as *Modern Drummer* and *Drums & Percussion.*

As a drum instructor, he teaches at the German university, Hochschule für Musik und Darstellende Kunst, in Frankfurt. He is the first European to receive a Distinguished Professor title from Keimyung University in Daegu, South Korea. Claus endorses Mapex Drums, Sabian Cymbals, Evans Drumheads, Promark Drumsticks, and Cooperman Rope Tension Drums. Learn more about Claus by visiting claushessler.com.

Preface

There are two major reasons for writing this book. First, I wanted to shed a little more light on the many not-so-well-known facts about the origins of rudiments, which many of today's drummers don't know much about. Though most top drummers would say that a basic study of the rudiments is an important foundation of their art form, their history and European roots are in danger of being forgotten. Second, I hope to awaken an interest and passion for this special field of drumming that has had a massive influence on the way modern drumset playing has evolved. Most of the tunes throughout the book have been taken from the U.S. Camp & Garrison Duty—hence the title, *Claus Hessler's Camp Duty Update.*

When teaching, I often find that no stylistically adequate musical imagination goes into the rendition of a special pattern or tune, particularly regarding the choice of tempo, sound, and phrasing. Alternatively, when there is an attempt at interpretation, there is often interference from other musical influences that have nothing at all to do with the "original" sound. Just as jazz and certain forms of Latin music have their special characteristics and touch, so, too, do the different schools of rudimental traditions have distinguishing stylistic features. Their musical performance can only truly be authentic when these are observed. When it comes to rudiments (the core of our drumming world), we somehow neglect these considerations and seem to be content with instructional books or a poster on the wall of our rehearsal studio, rather than thinking about how the music is supposed to sound.

By examining several historical stages of rudimental drumming, I have tried to add more understanding to the field. During my research for this book, I came across many interesting facts, almost keeping me from executing my true intention—to help people improve their skills with rudiments. I hope to have found a reasonable compromise by also focusing on the music that would accompany the drumming. That said, another important goal has been to avoid limiting the book to superficial details that might then be misleading for future genera- tions of drummers.

The traditional pieces in this book can, of course, be understood as milestones of drumming, sometimes dating back 200 years and more; usually both the drum parts and melodies have evolved over time. Although many of the ancient versions are quite simple in structure, it seems that these need particular attention and care when it comes to creating a true musical rendition. My own interpretations (the "Another" versions, which can be heard on the accompanying CD) are mostly influenced by Basel drumming, French traditional elements, and contem- porary American rudimental drumming. I have found that many of the more traditional patterns gain clarity and musical flow once you start considering an underlying rhythmic structure of quintuplets. You are encouraged to refer to the additional exercises in the → *appendix* (which follow the same structure as the ones in my book *Daily Drumset Workout*).

See pp. 73.

A few words regarding the recording: The play-alongs with a real fife will help to add more musical authenticity; each version of the tunes also comes with a slightly slowed-down version. Also, every track has a click counting you in. This way you can also practice playing along with my rendition on the recording. You could even make it a duo performance with yourself playing the original score and me playing the "Another" version—or vice versa.

Two more things before we get going:

Any style of music and any written piece of music are open to individual interpretation, and the tunes in this book are no different. I tried to find a form of notation that is as true to the intended sound as possible, conveying the structure in the best possible way and yet remaining easy to read and understand.

Secondly, you don't have to have a real field drum in order to make use of this material; you can, of course, also just use a regular snare! I am closing this preface with a statement I found during the research for this book. It combines basically everything that drumming is about to me:

"... take pride in making it look easy and beat your duty with spirit!"

Claus Hessler
www.claushessler.com

Contents

MP3 Recording

All tracks have a four-bar count-off. On tunes in $\frac{2}{4}$ time, the BPM-info relates to the quarter notes; on tunes in $\frac{6}{8}$ time the tempo information relates to the dotted quarter notes.

01	Air des Fifres ou Hautbois	82 BPM	00:52
02	Air des Fifres ou Hautbois—Roulée	82 BPM	00:52
03	Air des Fifres ou Hautbois—Play-Along	82 BPM	00:52
04	Air des Fifres ou Hautbois—Play-Along slow		00:58
05	Three Camps	110 BPM	01:11
06	Another Three Camps	110 BPM	01:11
07	Three Camps—Play-Along	110 BPM	01:10
08	Three Camps—Play-Along slow		01:17
09	Breakfast Call	118 BPM	00:39
10	Another Breakfast Call	118 BPM	00:39
11	Breakfast Call—Play-Along	118 BPM	00:39
12	Breakfast Call—Play-Along slow		00:43
13	Dinner Call	84 BPM	00:36
14	Another Dinner Call	84 BPM	00:36
15	Dinner Call—Play-Along	84 BPM	00:36
16	Dinner Call—Play-Along slow		00:40
17	Dusky Night—Original Version No. 1	86 BPM	00:46
18	Dusky Night—Original Version No. 2	86 BPM	00:46
19	Another Dusky Night	86 BPM	00:46
20	Dusky Night—Play-Along	86 BPM	00:46
21	Dusky Night—Play-Along slow		00:51
22	The Slow Scotch	96 BPM	01:37
23	The Slow Scotch—Play-Along	96 BPM	01:37
24	The Slow Scotch—Play-Along slow		01:48
25	Another Slow Scotch	96 BPM	02:12
26	Another Slow Scotch—Play-Along	96 BPM	02:11
27	Another Slow Scotch—Play-Along slow		02:26
28	The Downfall of Paris	98 BPM	02:05
29	Another Downfall	98 BPM	02:05
30	The Downfall of Paris—Play-Along	98 BPM	02:05
31	The Downfall of Paris—Play-Along slow		02:19
32	Garryowen	112 BPM	01:19
33	Garryowen Play-Along	112 BPM	01:19
34	Garryowen—Play-Along slow		01:28
35	Another Garryowen	112 BPM	01:00
36	Another Garryowen—Play-Along	112 BPM	00:58
37	Another Garryowen—Play-Along slow		01:05
38	Dixie	98 BPM	01:46
39	Another Dixie	98 BPM	01:46
40	Dixie—Play-Along	98 BPM	01:46
41	Dixie—Play-Along slow		01:57
42	Yankee Doodle	108 BPM	01:00
43	Another Yankee Doodle	108 BPM	01:00
44	Yankee Doodle—Play-Along	108 BPM	01:00
45	Yankee Doodle—Play-Along slow		01:07
46	British Grenadiers	95 BPM	00:48
47	Another Grenadier	95 BPM	00:48
48	British Grenadiers—Play-Along	95 BPM	00:48
49	British Grenadiers—Play-Along slow		00:53

Matthias Dörsam: Piccolo Fife | Claus Hessler: Cooperman Rope Tension Drum

Notation

1. *Right-hand strokes* are notated above the line, and *left-hand strokes* below the line. Left-handed players can just reverse this if they wish.

2. For flams we use an abbreviated form using a little line inside the notehead. This applies both to single strokes and rolls:

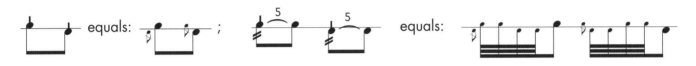

See pp. 21.

3. Drags | 3-stroke rolls are mostly written using traditional notation. Their interpretation tends very "open" (also see remarks on the drag in → *chapter 1*).

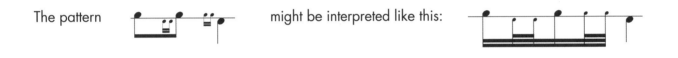

The pattern   might be interpreted like this:

See pp. 73.

See pp. 79.

4. With rolls we frequently make use of unusual rhythmic layers; check out the two examples as well as → *appendices 1 and 2*. In certain cases I also gave additional information in connection with the pieces themselves.

A 9-stroke roll e.g.,   is meant to be played like this:

There is also room for interpretation like this:

The phrase   should be played like this:

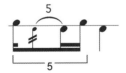

5. Sometimes it was difficult to show a "roll-like" phrase using abbreviated notation. In certain cases I have thus chosen to write patterns using noteheads of different sizes, which also improves the readability of the phrase:

Example 1:   Example 2:

CHAPTER 1 | HISTORY AND BACKGROUND

It was at a pretty early stage in preparing this book when I came to realize that it would not just be about the tunes themselves, but also about painting a picture of the vast culture of rudimental drumming, its history, and its evolution.

Every now and then, for example, my students will hear me say, "Know your enemies!" when it comes to working intensively on a rudiment or pattern. This is a statement made in jest, of course, but what I mean is that you need to know the background of what you are learning. This takes us to the very first question: *What really is a rudiment?*

RUDIMENTS: A DEFINITION

The word *rudiment* is actually of Latin descent; *rudimentum* literally means a first attempt or test run. The *rudis*, for instance, was a wooden sword used by gladiators for training purposes. Today we have different uses for this term, the most common ones being:

- A leftover, or fragment.
- In medical terms, something that is underdeveloped or unused (e.g., human hair, caecum, fingernails).
- The basic or elementary principles of a certain matter or issue.

For the purpose of this book I'd like to use this definition of rudiments:

DEFINITION

Rudiments are mostly fragments of tunes from the *Camp Duty* of the U.S., originally based on European drumming traditions. In the proper sense a rudiment today is an excerpt of a traditional military "march" or "call" with (more or less):

- defined rhythm
- defined dynamic structure
- defined sticking
- defined nomenclature.

The names of the phrases are often onomatopoeic (meaning they emulate the original sound) e.g., paradiddle, ratamacue, flam, pataflafla). Sometimes the names also refer to the structure of the phrase (e.g., five-stroke roll, double drag tap). The first agreement on 26 basic rudiments was reached in 1933 by the *National Association of Rudimental Drummers (NARD)* and was mostly based on prior literature (Strube, Ashworth, Potter; see → *appendix 3: sources and material used*).

See pp. 85.

Rudiments have always been connected to the evolution of the (snare) drum and its use in the military. The relevant literature makes several references to the fact that the crusades brought significant stimulus to Europe, both relating to drumming style and the instruments used. This also seems to be the reason why it was mostly the crusading nations who developed some kind of rudimental drumming tradition.

Drums and flags have always been regarded as superior trophies of war and retained their special significance well into modern times. Even in *World War II* there are reports recording that all efforts would be made to avoid the capturing of drums by the enemy. Of course, the very first evidence of drumming dates back to around 30,000 years ago. For us drummers, however, things start to get interesting somewhere around the medieval times. Switzerland and the neighboring French and German regions were of particular importance, but the records also include early references to Italy, England, and Prussia, as well as the Dutch provinces.

HISTORY OF RUDIMENTS: COMPRESSED TIMELINE

14TH CENTURY

In the 14th century, Switzerland was extremely influential in the development of the art of drumming. Sources mention of the use of drums (and fifes) there from the early part of the century (e.g., in connection with the Battle of Laupen in 1339). There are also references to the use of drums and fifes in the famous Battle of Sempach, although according to my research, there are no concrete records describing how drums were played and with what patterns. Just as with most other forms of early military music, psychological warfare must also have played a major role; the drums were supposed to encourage the soldiers while trying to frighten the foe. The painting *Prayer and Sermon of the Berns and Their Allies before the Battle of Laupen in 1339*, illustrated by the pictorial

chronicler Diebold Schilling the Younger, shows a soldier with a drum. As Schilling found the drum necessary to include in the picture, it must have had a certain significance in warfare. However, the chronicler couldn't have been a true contemporary witness—he was only born around the middle of the 15th century (there are no records about the exact year) and most likely died in Lucerne in 1515. Therefore, it is difficult to say if his picture really illustrates the exact spirit and fashion of 1339 or of his age. On the other hand, it is fair to assume that this era did not progress so quickly that such customs would have changed drastically in a short space of time.

Anyhow, using that kind of illustration as evidence for the exclusive use of drums in Switzerland would be taking it too far. Other works of Schilling featuring drumming and fifing bears (also used in connection with the Battle of Laupen) do at least outline the basic connection of these two instruments with warfare. Recordings also refer to the military use of drums in England in the 14th century during the Second War of Scottish Independence. Poems and ballads referring to the victory of the English over the Scottish under King Edward III at Halidon Hill mention the use of so-called tabers. When we hear the terms *taber* or *tabor*, however, we usually think of drums of a somewhat smaller size than those in the illustrations of Diebold Schilling. A typical technique would be to play the drum with one hand and at the same time a fife with the other hand, both instruments thus being played by the same person. However we cannot be sure if the English drums were of the same size and construction as the ones in Switzerland.

Long story short, the first evidence of the use of fifes and drums in connection with military and profane, secular functions can be found in Switzerland, as well as in England, as early as the 14th century. The Swiss therefore can definitely claim to be a very significant—but not the only—source of the rudiments as we know them today. A lot of relevant history can also be found in France, which we will hear about soon.

Burger Library Bern, Mss.h.h.I.16, p. 270 & Mss.h.h.I.16, p. 227
photos: Codices Electronici AG, www.e-codices.ch

15TH CENTURY

First evidence of the special connection between Fasnacht (the Swiss Carnival) and drumming can be found in administrative orders dating back to 1422 that banned masqueraded mercenaries from milling around with drums. The corresponding decree was also aimed at "foreign mercenaries" (for instance, from adjacent areas in today's Germany) and not just at Swiss soldiers alone. Official records from 1445 show that certain drum signals were used to call the inhabitants to arms in Basel, Switzerland; before that, a call to arms was most likely organized through trumpet calls and by ringing church bells.

As previously mentioned, the use of drums was most likely not strictly exclusive to Switzerland. Swiss mercenaries, however, could be found at numerous princely houses throughout Europe. Their travels were, then, also responsible for the dissemination of their accessories—which include the Swiss fife and drum (Schwyzer Pfeiff und Trummel) along with certain signals and marches. In 1492, for example, Sweche grete taborers (meaning Swiss people with big drums) were on the payroll of English King Henry VII. There is a good chance that this Swiss influence could be the reason why both the English and Swiss marches have tended to be rather solemn and on the slow side.

Swiss soldiers also had a strong presence in France, most likely how the subsequent special drumming relationship between these two nations began. The so-called Cent Suisses or the Gardes du Corps Suisse had a special responsibility for the security of the French kings and the royal residences. A French royal decree from 1656 would later designate a typical line-up of the royal lifeguards as three drummers and one fifer. Later still, in the 19th century, the Swiss were using a "General" march with French roots (La generalle de la garde françoise).

16TH CENTURY

The 16th century marked the arrival of a true Renaissance highlight for drumming. In 1588 Thoinot Arbeau from Dijon produced his *Orchésographie*. His book is truly one of the most remarkable works of this era, providing amazingly detailed and systematic information about the rhythmic structure of certain drumming patterns. Among other fascinating background details, Arbeau describes the preferred typical basic beat of French drummers at that time, as follows:

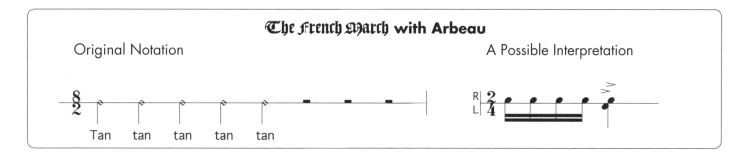

The complete pattern is made up of eight half notes (Arbeau expressly mentions *minims*), with the pulse or beat on the first and fifth units. Beats 1 and 5 then also establish the tempo the soldiers should march at. Arbeau mentions that the first four strokes are to be played with only one hand (unfortunately, he doesn't let us know which), and the fifth minim using both hands. It is likely that this represents an early form of a flam or Coup de Charge in the Swiss nomenclature, though it may really have been intended that both hands should move in unison. My version is thus somewhat speculative. Arbeau also describes the preferred style of the Swiss drummers, a characteristic being to leave out the note on beat 4. This Swiss March did not have a special fife melody or theme, but, nevertheless, the typical structure of the march must have been enough to identify Swiss army units. Verbalizing "colin tan plon" seems to have served as a kind of methodical memory aid.

It seems as though the accent played with both hands on beat 5 has been retained in today's pattern:

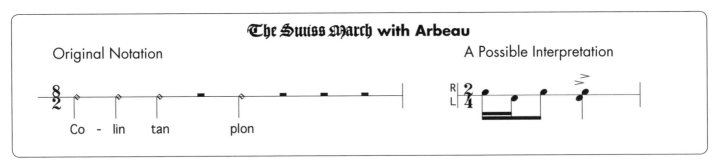

Arbeau also addresses how and why soldiers were to march in step and works with the use of certain syllables to resemble patterns in the French and Swiss styles (e.g., *tan-tan-fre-tere-tan*). The box below shows some of his examples in the French style, which are also relevant to the first tune in this book. The syllable *fre* has a roll-like texture, but the text does not give any information on how the rolls should be played (double strokes, single strokes, closed rolls). I assume some kind of five-stroke roll is represented here, shown in the interpretation on the right side of the table below. Regarding the execution, my guess is that the interpretation is almost some kind of mixture of open and closed roll—not really a strong double-stroke RRLL action, but not a pressing of the sticks into the drumhead either.

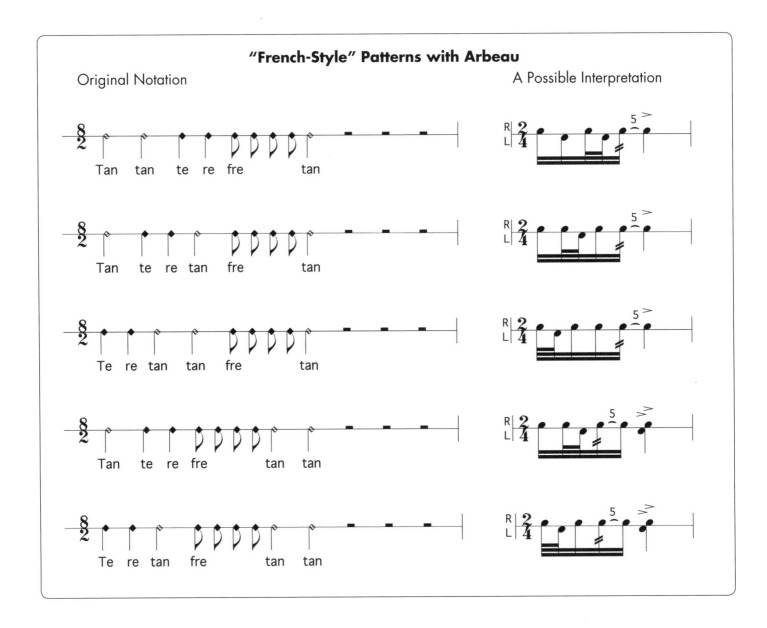

17TH CENTURY

In English records from the 17th century there are some remarkable statements concerning the importance and function of drums in their military use. There is reference to so-called *drumsleds* or *drumslades* (literally meaning *drumbeaters*). In his *Five Decades of Epistles of Warre* from 1622 Francis Markham writes:

> "The Phiph is but only an instrument of pleasure, and not of necessity, and it is to the voice of the Drumme the soldier should wholly attend . . . the Drumme being the very tongue and voice of the Commander, he is to have an exceeding careful and diligent ear. If he beat a retreat when commanded to Charge, or to beat a Charge when men are to retire, the army might perish by the action. The soldier must be diligent and learn all the beatings of the Drumme . . . and how they differ in their significations."

Markham's statement mirrors the traditional French structure and organization of drums and fifes in the 17th century—the relevant voice carrying the military order is the drum—not the fife. Looking at this from today's standpoint it might seem surprising that the flutes accompany the drums and not the other way around. (*Note:* In the French cavalry, which used timpani and trumpets, the structure was reversed—the timpani accompanied the trumpets, with the military order contained in the voice of the trumpets.) The field drums of this period must have been pretty large instruments, as evidenced by contemporary pictures and engravings by Marine Mersenne (*Harmonie Universelle*), Michael Praetorius (*Syntagma Musicum*), or also as the antique, surviving instruments show. As a rule they seem to have had a diameter of between 18 and 20 inches, and the shell had a similar depth (sometimes even more). In some cases these drums even measured 24 inches in diameter.

In keeping with the *Swiss March*, the *English March* is thought to have consisted predominantly of a characteristic drum part without a proper flute melody; interestingly enough, both pieces were thought to have been lost for good at different times since. The famous *Warrant* of Charles I from 1632 demands that this march should be played with its original majestic gravity. Obviously, Charles wanted this piece to be played again in its true form. The original document has unfortunately been lost. However a couple of copies still exist, as do different works regarding the original interpretation of the *English March*. The text of the *Warrant* commences with these words:

> "Whereas the ancient custome of nations hath ever bene to use one certaine and constant forme of March in the warres, whereby to be distinguished one from another. And the March of this our nation, so famous in all the honourable achievements and glorious warres of this our kingdom in forraign parts (being by the approbation of strangers themselves confest and acknowledged the best of all marches) was through the negligence and carelessness of drummers and by long discontinuance so altered and changed from the ancient gravity and majestie thereof, as it was in danger utterly to have bene lost and forgotten."

Records also show that different regions' and nations' military units could be recognized by their drumming styles and their marches and beats. There are several British 15th-century documents that mention the following marches:

Th'enlish Marche	(The English March)
Th'allmaigne Marche	(The German March)
The flemish Marche	(The Flemish March)
The frenche Marche	(The French March)
The Pyemonnt Marche	(The Piedmontese March)

to name just a few.

The notation is reminiscent of Arbeau and also includes additional information underneath the music. With Arbeau we find the use of onomatopoeia (*tan tere tan*, etc.), whereas here there is more of an attempt to describe the execution itself in a more detailed way. The syllables *pou* and *tou* most likely represent the sticking indication: *Pou* meaning a right-hand stroke, while *tou* stands for the left hand. (*Author's note*: The *pou* and *tou* indicators for the order of strokes can still be found in Levi Lovering's *Drummers' Assistant or The Art of Drumming Made Easy* from 1818. Presumably there might also be a connection with the term *Flam-a-poo*, describing a *Flam Tap*.) Most historians indicate the capital R as a roll, yet its detailed execution is hardly reconstructable. The term *Poung* might be an early version of the *Poing Stroke* or *Pong Stroke*, which can also be found in early American drum notation; both pose a conundrum regarding the execution. It seems very likely that they stand for an accented stroke by means of an ancient rimshot, hitting the drum and the wooden tensioning hoop at the same time. The problem, however, is that most of the sources that describe this stroke refer to a rimshot played by both hands (in fact a flammed rimshot). Playing a flam after a preceding roll (as shown in the following example) seems unlikely, though, unless you allow for an additional, very short rest in between.

The *English March* consisted of two parts: The *Voluntary Before The March*, played first, and then *The March*. The *Voluntary Before The March* has no detailed time signature, nor is there any reliable indication of the tempo this sequence would be played at.

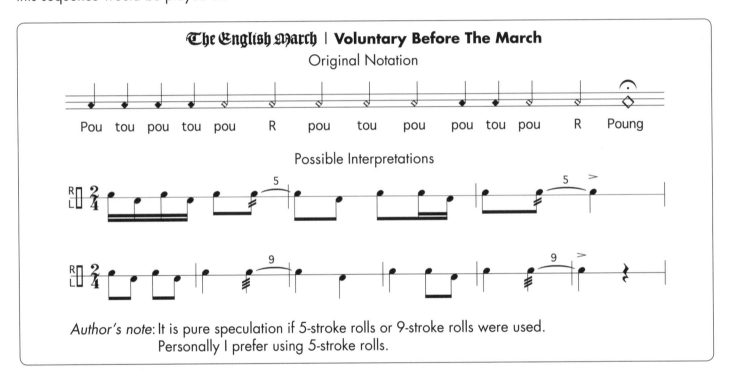

The English March | Voluntary Before The March
Original Notation

Pou tou pou tou pou R pou tou pou pou tou pou R Poung

Possible Interpretations

Author's note: It is pure speculation if 5-stroke rolls or 9-stroke rolls were used.
Personally I prefer using 5-stroke rolls.

Variations of some of the patterns included in the *Voluntary Before The March* were then included in *The March*. Thus, the *English March* consisted of several parts. The major part follows the structure that Arbeau describes as the *French style*, made up of five strokes of which the fifth was accented. An interesting development can be found here in that sticking is indicated, whereas in Arbeau's version it is not. Performing the *Poung* as kind of a *rimshot flam*, using both hands, would be possible technically:

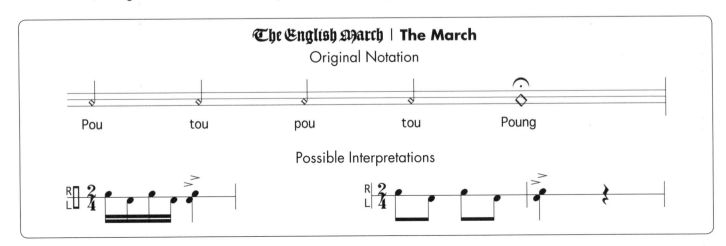

The English March | The March
Original Notation

Pou tou pou tou Poung

Possible Interpretations

Interpreting the *English March* in the historically proper way and uncovering all its hidden or forgotten details have been constant challenges for historians. Thus the different attempts and interpretations have always been notional to a certain degree.

The first emigrants to the *New World*—what would later become the United States of America—also exported their drums and drumming there. In 1637 Arthur Perry, who was a type of town crier, would announce news, the beginning of religious services, and anything that would be of interest for the people of Boston, by beating his drum accordingly. This instrument is now a museum object and the oldest still existing drum in the U.S. The first professional drummers (if you want to call them that) will most likely have been the bellmen of the first settlements of English emigrants.

From here, let's focus a little more on what was happening in the U.S. and see what happened to the European roots of drumming in the *New World*.

18TH CENTURY

In this era, the *War of Independence* (also called the *Revolutionary War* [1775–1783]) between the new colonies and Great Britain had a major impact on American military music and drumming, including how the patterns—later known as rudiments—would develop. At this time, Swiss mercenaries were still spreading their art of drumming all over Europe; besides farming and skilled crafts and trades, Swiss soldiers remained a major export for the country. There is evidence that approximately 40,000 Swiss mercenaries were fighting under foreign flags around the time when the French Revolution started, thus spreading their way of drumming. In 1792, however, the royal lifeguard of the French kings (remember the →*Cent Suisses*) was disbanded by Louis XVI. Those soldiers who still possessed Swiss citizenship returned to their homes; many others stayed but later died during the attack on the Tuileris on August 10, 1792, or were captured and beheaded by guillotine. The *Lions' Monument* in Lucerne, Switzerland, reminds us of the Swiss mercenaries of the *Gardes Suisses* who were killed in action.

↑ See pp. 9.

During this era the British Army introduced their *Camp and Garrison Duty*. This collection of tunes, calls, and signals played a major role in the daily routine of the soldiers by helping to structure and announce any event between the wake-up call and the tattoo. In Germany a book with the suggestive title *Kurze Anweisung das Trommel-Spielen auf die leichteste Art zu erlernen* (translation: *A Short Instruction on How to Learn to Play the Drums in the Easiest Way*) was published. Besides some basic musical and technical information, it contains a number of beats used in the military such as the so-called *reveille* (the wake-up call for troops), which already shows significant similarities to structures that can also be found in the equivalent Swiss *Tagwacht* or the *Diane* in the French drumming tradition: the typical combination of a 9-stroke roll and a structure similar to a double drag tap. However, the 3-stroke rolls (ruffs/drags) are missing. Unfortunately, neither the text nor the notation in the book clarify in any detail how the rolls should be played. The assignment shown in the text below is, of course, also composed in an old form of German, which I have tried to preserve in my translation:

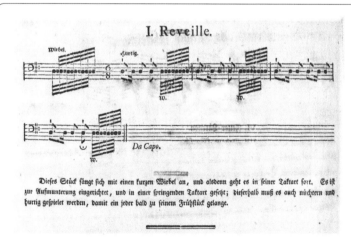

"Dieses Stück fängt sich mit einen kurzen Wirbel an, und alsdenn geht es in seiner Taktart fort. Es ist zur Aufmunterung eingerichtet, und in einer springenden Taktart gesetzt; dieserhalb muß es auch nüchtern und hurtig gespielet werden, damit ein jeder bald zu seinem Frühstück gelange.

"Dieses Stück fängt sich mit einem kurzen Wirbel an, und alsdenn geht es in seiner Taktart fort. Es ist zur Aufmunterung eingerichtet, und in einer springenden Taktart gesetzt; dieserhalb muss es auch nüchtern und hurtig gespielet werden, damit ein jeder bald zu seinem Frühstück gelange."

Author's translation: This piece starts with a short roll and moves on in the same measure. Played in a bouncy manner, it is meant to awaken people from their slumber and call them to a quick breakfast.

The book features onomatopoeic signals for the music (for instance *trau-lau-rau*) and a remarkable collection of *words of wisdom*, at times quite visionary in their quality:

> "**W**er kann es wiedersprechen, ob nicht nach einem Verlauf von hundert Jahren Concerte auf der Trommel gespielet werden? Im Hollsteinischen tanzen die gemeinen Leute Minuette und Angloisen nach der Trommel. Schon ein sehr weit gebrachter Anfang!"
>
> **Author's translation:** Who can tell if in a hundred years or more people will maybe even perform proper concerts on the drum? In Holstein [a region in northern Germany] people already dance minuets and angloises to the sound of the drum. That is already quite an achievement!

It seems likely that an anonymous author copied certain parts of this book in his own publication *Over het Tromslaan* (*About Beating the Drum*) in 1809; there is a good deal of overlap with the preceding German book, which was released in 1801.

The new American colonies introduced their "Regulations," which were approved by the Continental Congress in Philadelphia. These regulations were written instructions by Friedrich von Steuben, a former Prussian officer who became famous for his special drill phase in Valley Forge, educating officers for the American Continental Army. Rather than showing any music or notes, however, these "Regulations" describe the drumming more or less verbally:

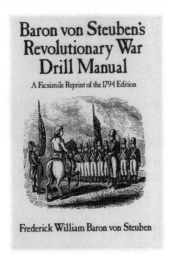

> "... for the front to advance quicker—the long march. To march slower—the taps. Front halt—two flams from right to left, and a full drag with the right, a left hand flam and a right hand full drag ..."

Frederick W. Baron Von Steuben: *Baron Von Steuben's Revolutionary War Drill Manual*
Facsimile edition available by Dover Books on Americana; ISBN 978-0486249346

An instruction like this is still vague, as detailed information about what should be played with which hand is still missing, though this doesn't automatically mean that there was no order or predefinition at all.

The *Supreme Commander of the Continental Army*, George Washington, was well aware of the importance and the function of drummers in the military. He also knew that his army was more an accumulation of ambitious civilians rather than real soldiers, and being well trained in the art of warfare he also realized that in the *War of Independence* he was facing one of the most powerful armed forces in the world of that time. It might be exactly for this reason that he appreciated the drums and fifes so much, with their motivating power and influence on the mood and mental condition of the soldiers. This recorded order given by Washington speaks volumes:

> "**T**he music of the army being in general very bad, it is expected, that the drum and fife majors exert themselves to improve it, or they will be reduced and their extraordinary pay taken from them. Stated hours are to be assigned, for all the drums and fifes, of each regiment, to attend them and practice. Nothing is more agreeable, and ornamental, than good music, every officer, for the credit of his corps, should take care to provide it..."

Marching with fifes and drums, and defining the tempos and number of steps involved, also served as a kind of rangefinder for troop movements and thus was a significant aid in making strategic military calculations.
It would be the commanders who determined the marches and the step tempo. The *Prussian Step* must have been somewhere around 60–70 BPM, *The Grand March* around 80 BPM, *Common Time Marches* around 96 BPM, and *Quick Time* approximately around 120 BPM.

Thus, the drums were vital in ensuring that the troops would march at a constant tempo over a certain period of time, which allowed more precise forecasts regarding the coverage of distance. Drums and fifes were also important over short distances. A bayonet attack, for instance, was initiated at a distance of around 1,000 yards from the enemy. Here the troops would stop and the bayonets would be attached to the rifles. In order to demonstrate strict discipline and strength of nerve, the soldiers would then march another 400 yards with the slow *Prussian*. After that the commanders usually ordered an advance of around 200 yards in *The Grand March*, then used *Common Time* for the next 200 yards, then another 100 yards in *Quick Time*, etc., until at the final clash of lines the tempo was raised again, sometimes even doubled. Any miscalculation of distances, tempo, and rifle range could be fatal, possibly weakening the frontline to a degree where the success of the attack was put in doubt.

Verbal and onomatopoeic instructions also dominated in Switzerland during the 1700s. Here is an excerpt from a Swiss 1788 drum duty, entitled *Die erste Tagwacht* (meaning *The Reveille*). The sound of the rolls is imitated with the words *Rrrang-rrangrang*, etc.:

Die erste Tagwacht

Zu jedem Takt von dieser Ordonnanz gehört ein Schritt. Man wird stets, sowohl die erste als die zweyte Partie, zweimal hintereinander schlagen. Die rechte Hand macht das vorzügliche Spiel von dieser Tagwacht.

Rrrang	rrangrang	Rrrang	rrangrang
Rrrang	rrangrang	Rrrang	rrangrang : :
Rrangrang		rrrangrang	rrrangrang
ratatangtang		Rrrangrang	ratatangtang
ratatangtang		ratatatatang : :

"...Zu jedem Takt von dieser Ordonnanz gehört ein Schritt. Man wird stets, sowohl die erste als die zweyte Partie, zweimal hinter einander schlagen. Die rechte Hand macht das vorzügliche Spiel von dieser Tagwacht."

Translation: Every bar of this ordinance relates to one step. You will always play the first and the second part twice. The right hand dominates the performance of this reveille.

"Tagwacht" (Image by Claus Hessler)

This strategy of imitating the sounds of the drums can be found to this very day in Basel drumming and is also described in the methods of Dr. Fritz Berger, one of the grand masters of Swiss drumming. It might sound funny to our ears today, but it can definitely be of great help as a memory aid and assist in developing a notion of the sound that you are about to produce. And haven't we come across this aspect already with the →*Orchésographie*?

See pp. 9.

19TH CENTURY

The American *Civil War* (1861–1865) was undoubtedly one of the most formative events for the configuration and further development of military music and drumming in the U.S. in the 19th century. During this time we also find an increasing amount of more detailed information and some of the first educational books that, in a more concrete way, tried to teach people what to do with which hand. One of the first true drum methods dates back to 1812: *A New, Useful and Complete System of Drum Beating* written by Charles Ashworth (who was an Englishman by the way). He uses the term *rudiment* in his writing and notates 27 basic patterns (quite close to 26!) by using a writing system that may look a little exotic from today's standpoint (e.g., he uses different noteheads for different dynamics, left-hand strokes are written higher in the five-line system than right-hand strokes, etc.). Ashworth also mentions patterns that are surprisingly close to some Swiss rudiments but which can't be found anymore in the American list of rudiments (see also the comparative list of rudiments and their names/origins in the →*appendix*). As already mentioned, Ashworth also tries to communicate dynamics in the way the noteheads are designed. In fact you can hardly find any common terms indicating dynamics such as piano, mezzoforte, forte, etc.; instead there are descriptions like *Faint Stroke* or *Faint Roll* whose noteheads look like half notes, for instance. He also describes proper grip using unique comparisons:

See pp. 73.

> *"... the left stick must be firmly held between the thumb and two middle fingers, to rest on the third finger a little above the middle joint. The right hand stick must be held fast by the little finger, and be allowed to play with ease through the others, as a man may use a stick in fencing."*

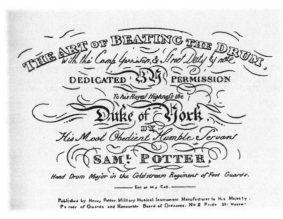

Samuel Potter's *The Art of Beating the Drum* (1817)
Reprint available at http://www.beafifer.com

Obviously Ashworth is describing something that Sanford Moeller taught a little more than one hundred years later. This feature of his famous technique was called the *little finger hold* (the technique was itself, of course, derived from Army veterans and not really Moeller's invention). Ashworth's book also includes a collection of important signals, calls, and marches for the military service including short descriptions for their use.

Soon after that we encounter another educational book by Samuel Potter (1772–1838) that leans heavily on Ashworth's book. His book gives further and more detailed information, although some of the details might possibly be questionable from today's perspective (especially those where he focuses on posture, for instance). Of course, I am not trying to belittle his work—I am just doubtful if some of his advice really has anything to do with a natural and relaxed playing position. Potter was the *Drum Major of the Coldstream Regiment of Foot Guards* and published three more books with tunes, as well as an instructional method for bugle and fifes. His work uses a modified system of writing that indicated left-hand and right-hand strokes in different positions of the five-line system, and employs terms that are no longer in use today, such as the *close flam* (meaning a flam as we understand it today with a close distance between grace note and main note, the grace note being soft) and the *open flam* (meaning a flam in which both strokes would be accented, thus being a sort of *coup de charge* in the Swiss nomenclature). We also hear about *flam and faint* (basically a *flam tap*, but with a larger distance between the strokes), *drag and stroke* (very similar to the single drag tap), the *mother* (our five-stroke roll today), and many more.

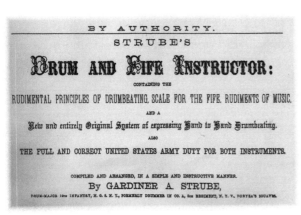

Strube's *Drum and Fife Instructor* (1869)
Reprint available at http://www.beafifer.com

More books followed: In 1862 came the famous and highly regarded *The Drummers' and Fifers' Guide* written by George B. Bruce and Daniel Emmett. Bruce served as a drummer in the U.S. Army while Emmett played the flute (after his time in the army he became a successful comedian and multi-instrumentalist in several minstrel shows—a remarkable combination). Just like many other notable methods around this time, their book is also separated into two halves: One part deals with the drumming, while the second half gives training for the flute/fife. Besides showing the rudiments it also has the *Camp Duty*, including detailed information about the use of the pieces and several more tunes and quicksteps for fife and drum with clear and easy-to-read notation. As well as the well-known *Old Dan Tucker*, Emmett was the composer of

See
pp. 58. the famous tune →"Dixie" (also known as "Dixieland," composed in 1860), which is especially associated with the American South (more on that later).

The first publication that mentions 26 basic rudiments is *Strube's Drum and Fife Instructor* (still called *lessons* in this book) by Gardiner A. Strube, written in 1869. In the same year the U.S. government acknowledged this method as the prevailing foundation for all Army drummers. Although the single-stroke roll is not a numbered rudiment, it is, of course, part of the 26 patterns. An essential fact is that the rudiments came into life as excerpts of military tunes and signals—not the other way around. To this day the common misconception prevails that military drum music was constructed using rudiments, which is definitely not the case.

Just as French military music switched from fifes to oboes around the end of the 17th century, we find a shift from fifes to bugles in the U.S. in the 19th century. At the time that these bugles (trumpets without valves) were introduced we find another important publication in 1880: John Philip Sousa's *A Book Instruction for Field Trumpet and Drum*. One of Sousa's drummers, August Helmicke, was later to become one of the first formal teachers of Sanford Augustus Moeller. After Helmicke, the famous George L. Stone also went on to be a drummer in Sousa's Concert Band.

20TH CENTURY UNTIL TODAY...

In 1933 the newly founded NARD put together a collection of 26 rudiments that can be regarded as the first ever "official" list of rudiments. They are separated into 13 essential and 13 auxiliary patterns. When this selection of rudiments was drawn up the available literature would, of course, have been drawn upon. One important source was clearly *Strube's Drum and Fife Instructor*. Ashworth, Bruce & Emmett and Potter were certainly other major influences (please also refer to the →*appendix of sources* in this book).

See pp. 85.

George Lawrence Stone and most of his fellow drum instructors of the time (e.g., Sanford Moeller or William "Billy" Gladstone) strongly stressed having a relaxed, loose execution and emphasized the power of rebound. They may have had different terms for a rebounding stroke (*free stroke, stop at the top, catching the bounce*, etc.), but they all urged their students not to hold down the sticks after impact. Some of Stone's students include legendary players Vic Firth, "Big" Sid Catlett, Lionel Hampton, Gene Krupa, Ted Reed, and, of course, Joe Morello. While Stone was predominantly a classical drummer, he still had a soft spot for modern drumset playing. He was well acquainted with the tradition of American rudimental drumming and also one of the few drummers not inherently against the use of matched grip. Here is a passage from an article published in the *International Musician Magazine* in January 1948:

> "...We hold our left drumstick differently from our right because our forefathers did so... they did this because they were marching drummers and their drum, suspended by a shoulder strap, naturally hung at an angle as they marched."

The Moeller Book: The Art of Snare Drumming (published in 1956) can be seen as a continuation of traditional drumming values with a more modern look, indicating up and down strokes using corresponding symbols, for instance. (*Author's note*: A number of these symbols could in fact be questioned regarding correctness.) Although the title of the book may suggest that it holds information about Moeller's famous technique (or "system," as some of his students also called it), there is little insight into the technical strategies used by the Army veterans that Moeller watched. Instead, there is information about musical/drumming basics and exercises and the *Camp Duty of the U.S. Army*, plus a selection of well-known pieces for fife and drum including the fife notation (e.g., "Dixie" or "The

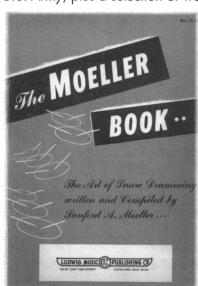

Downfall of Paris"). Moeller was serious about the preservation of the rudiments and their adequate and correct interpretation in the traditional way, and became famous for his 250-mile march to Boston—drumming every step of the distance. His observations of veterans who had served in the *Civil War* later became the initial spark for what is known today as the *Moeller Technique*; he was strongly influenced by the drumming tradition in the style of Bruce & Emmett. He also made his own rope tension field drums and taught ensembles and drum corps in the traditional style of drumming, his most famous students including Gene Krupa and James Forbes Chapin (better known as Jim Chapin), the father of modern drumset independence and another proponent of Moeller's technique.

The Moeller Book by Sanford A. Moeller
Item-#: 10300106 Ludwig Masters Publications,
Boca Raton, FL, U.S.A.

Authors/instructors like Charley Wilcoxon, J. Burns Moore, or John S. Pratt also created new literature that is now a *must-have* in every drummer's library. Yet it appears that at a certain point the misconception developed that classic rudimental beats used in the military were created through the combination of different rudiments—which is not exactly true. The rudiments were, of course, used in these beats, signals, and marches, but the rudiments were more or less extracts and excerpts from the tunes. Nevertheless, it cannot be denied that drummers like Pratt and Wilcoxon gave this genre of drumming a very important new push.

Rudiments: Geographical and Musical Connections

There can be no doubt that there are areas and countries in which rudiments and the music connected with them have gained a special status. Similar to languages and their regional dialects or slang, there are different rudimental styles or schools within the field of drumming. Although it takes a little experience, there are a number of characteristic aspects that make a certain style of drumming unique and recognizable, such as the Swiss drumming style, French rudimental drumming, or Scottish pipe band drumming. Generally speaking the distinctions are based not only on the structure of the tunes themselves and the choice of patterns, but also on the differences in sound (which are mostly dependent on the drums and their individual characteristics). Other aspects include the choice of tempo and the phrasing of rolls and flams. In this section I would like to give you a short description of the most important and well-known rudimental schools.

The Swiss School of Drumming | Basel Drumming

The distinguishing features include the peculiarities of the Swiss drums and their sound, the typical phrasing and interpretation of pieces, as well as the use of patterns/rudiments that are not known or not very common in American rudimental drumming. A very special manifestation of Swiss drumming is known as *Basel drumming*, for which the the town of Basel and its surrounding area can be seen as a stronghold. Here, this type of drumming really is a form of popular sport, performed at an astonishingly high level. A particularly important event, for which Basel drumming forms an indispensable part, is the *Fasnacht* (the Swiss Carnival celebration comparable to the *Brazilian Carnival* or *New Orleans Mardi Gras*), held every year in Basel, including its opening ceremony, the *Morgenstreich*, which commences at 4 a.m. (The *Fasnacht* is particularly famous for its drum and fife tradition—for those of you who have not heard about it, check it out and be amazed by the artistry of the drummers and fifers and the rich cultural background of this unique event.)

There is an interesting mixture of customs connected with the Swiss Carnival and military ingredients in different genres of drumming pieces, be it traditional marches used for the *Fasnacht* (usually in connections with fifes), reveilles or *Tagwachten* (tunes to wake up people—comparable to the *Three Camps*, but usually much more complex), and retreats (*Retraite*). Traditional folk songs have also had a strong influence and have added to the wide spread acceptance of drumming traditions in the Swiss population. Throughout Switzerland there are musical drumming clubs and societies (so-called *cliques*). The list of big names in Basel drumming is headed by Dr. Fritz Berger and his master student Alfons Grieder, both of whom can be regarded as the international ambassadors of this genre of drumming, having built up international networks during their lifetimes. Dr. Berger is also known for the invention of a special form of notation for Basel drumming as well as for putting energy into the preservation of this unique art form.

The French School of Drumming

There are many similarities between the French school of rudimental drumming and Basel drumming. Over the centuries the two methods actively exchanged techniques, helping to enrich both drumming cultures. Just as in Basel drumming, the French prefer a fist-like grip in their right hand, while the left stick is held in what we would refer to as *traditional grip*. The technique developed from the position of the drum, which hung at the side of the player, suspended by a sling across the shoulder. Another parallel is the form of notation that is usually also a single-line system, the only difference being that the French write left-hand strokes above the line and right-hand strokes below the line, while the Swiss do the opposite. The Swiss and the French tradition also share a collection of rudiments that are hardly found in the American school of rudimental drumming. First of all, there is the frequent use of the so-called *coup anglais* (or the *doublé* in Basel drumming) and its characteristic phrasing. The rudiments known as *Endstreich* in Basel drumming (literally translated "final stroke"—a combination that is typical for the ending measure of a Swiss drumming verse, also used throughout any *Fasnacht* march) can also be found in the French drumming culture and might well have been the trigger for the adoption of these patterns in the Swiss culture. It is likely that returning Swiss soldiers formerly serving in French units imported or even re-imported certain rudiments. Some patterns also reveal their French ancestry by their name, such as the *pataflafla*, although the combination itself is understood differently to the American list of rudiments. Great names of French rudimental drumming include Alexandre Raynaud and Robert Goute.

The Traditional American School of Drumming

This is a drumming culture with its roots in European rudimental traditions. We find similar drums to those used in Basel drumming and the French school of rudimental drumming, using rope tension and sizes of about 16″ x 16″ (the sizes do differ, of course), calfskin heads, and gut snares. This genre of drumming is sometimes also referred to as the *Civil War* or *Revolutionary War* style. One significant trademark is the (more or less) *delayed* ending of certain rolls (mostly on 7-stroke rolls and 15-stroke rolls). This may sound awkward to people unfamiliar with this style of drumming, but it is in fact a very significant characteristic of it. Early sources and literature also feature right-hand and left-hand strokes notated at different heights in the line system, with left-hand strokes usually above right-hand strokes (similar to the French way of writing). The stems of the notes sometimes additionally help to indicate the sticking (left hand stems up, right hand stems down). Great names of American rudimental drumming include Sanford Moeller, Earl Sturtze, and J. Burns Moore.

The Scottish School of Drumming

As with American contemporary rudimental drumming (see below), the Scots use high tension snares—also referred to as *side drums* or *pipe drums* (since they are accompanied by the Scotch pipes). The drumheads are not calfskin but a highly resilient kind of kevlar material, and additional snares are often placed under the batter head. One distinguishing feature of Scottish pipe band drumming is the dominant use of closed rolls (which are not really used in the French, Swiss, or traditional American style). Another characteristic is the way drags are interpreted: the executing hand really presses the stick into the head, the stick remaining on the drumhead while the opposite hand plays the main note. The Swiss form of notation invented by Dr. Fritz Berger obviously inspired the Scots to use a single-line system as well; there are reports about an active exchange between Berger and Scottish Drum Major James Catherwood. Typical tunes are the *jig, hornpipe, reel,* and *strathspey*, which all have their special intricacies. Great names of the Scottish school of drumming are Alex Duthart and Jim Kilpatrick.

It is arguable that the schools and genres mentioned above, along with certain influences from the orchestral or classical styles of drumming, have helped to create another style of drumming that could be described as...

Contemporary Rudimental Drumming

This genre came into life at some point in the 1960s and is featured in modern drum corps and ensembles. It does not share too many parallels with the old method of American rudimental drumming, and the drums used here are very similar to those used in the Scottish system, featuring kevlar heads, the typical high tension sound, and heavy, big sticks. My mentor Jim Chapin sometimes used the term *kevlar kids* for the artists—which I don't necessarily see as a negative description. In this style of drumming we also find influences from Latin music, rock, pop, rap, and other artistic additions, including all kinds of stick tricks, etc. Great names of this genre would include players, educators, and instructors like John Wooton, Jeff Queen, or Ralph Hardimon.

FREQUENT MISCONCEPTIONS

It goes without saying that if you lack technique and/or skill it is always going to be difficult to realize your musical creativity, and this book is not intended to provide technical instruction in that sense; I would prefer that you view it as a helpful guide in how to interpret certain phrases in the most satisfactory way. The following aspects should be focused on most:

NO DIRECT LINK BETWEEN "CLASSICAL" DRUMMING AND "RUDIMENTAL" DRUMMING

None of the genres of rudimental drumming mentioned above have any special affinity with the features, qualities, and characteristics that can be found in the classical or orchestral methods of playing a snare drum. One frequent misconception would thus be to interpret a piece from Charley Wilcoxon's *All American Drummer* using the same guidelines and musical creativity as if it would be an etude of Goldenberg or Vic Firth. The school mentioned as *Contemporary Rudimental Drumming* (→*see the previous page*) might well draw from classical snare drumming in certain aspects, but even here we do not really play "classical" snare.

See
pp. 19.

The notion of sound and interpretation in orchestral drumming obviously differs from that of rudimental drumming. The reasons are manifold: Rudimental drumming is, of course, much older than classical drumming and the musical frame is totally different, just as the instruments are. A *Dresdner Trommel* (a typical German classical snare drum with a metal shell) is built very differently than an *American field drum* or *Basel drum*. And since
5" x 14" and 16" x 16" are obviously not the same dimensions, we also play these two instruments in a very different way, using different techniques, different dynamics, and so forth. The traditional schools of rudimental drumming tend not to use techniques in which rolls are played somewhere close to the edge of the drum to perform them with less volume—this, on the other hand, is a very common procedure in classical snare drumming. Another aspect of misinterpretation is the use of rim shots with players who have a drumset background—the traditional schools of rudimental drumming do not feature an extensive use of strokes that include rim sounds. The only exception would possibly be the ancient poing stroke as already described in connection with →*The English March* earlier in this book.

See
pp. 12.

CHOICE OF TEMPO

Adequate choice of tempo is another subject of misunderstanding. There is a wide range between "too slow" and "much too fast." Whenever your choice of tempo is in the "too fast" category, you have to understand that the range of options for musical expression will be narrowed down drastically. Generally speaking, many traditional pieces (no matter if they are of Swiss or American origin) tended to be played rather on the slow side than at faster tempos (in fact the choice of tempo is a major issue when it comes to distinguishing between ancient/traditional and modern performances). Considering the additional aspect of marching soldiers and drummers we should not forget that there are limits in terms of how long and fast men can march and still be ready to attack and defend themselves against an attack by the enemy. When marching across the country, the streets and roads would most likely not have allowed for faster marching tempos and the corresponding drumming. Back in the times of non-standardized gun calibers, all the tools, materials, and appliances had to be transported as well. The big *field drums* with their calfskin drumheads and climatic sensitivities would not have been able really to convey a clear articulation of strokes in very tight and close combinations either. The acoustic setting in conditions open to the elements would have been yet another aspect causing adverse circumstances.

Yet that is still is a far cry from saying that they only played at slow tempos back then. There would definitely have been players that pushed the limits and developed amazing technical dexterity. I am only saying that the lion's share of the daily drumming routine was most likely performed at a dignified, medium tempo. Too many ornaments and *fancy bits* were not always welcome either; a lot of evidence confirms that military drumming had to be largely easy to comprehend with a very functional approach. According to records, drummers used to determine tempos using a thread with a weight attached to it. The method of selecting a specific length of thread, bringing the weight (such as a musket ball) to a 90-degree angle, and then releasing it and watching the weight swing back and forth, would give a basic idea about tempo. (This was quite a common method between the late 17th century and the early 19th century, well before the invention of the metronome around 1815.)

THE DRAG | THE SWISS "DREIER RUF" | THE FRENCH "RA DE TROIS"...AND WHAT ABOUT THE RUFF?

One of the most frequent mistakes (especially in more traditional rudimental drumming) would be to leave too little space between the notes of phrases that make use of any sort of *drag* ingredients. In German orchestral nomenclature the drag is referred to as a kind of *doubled flam*; in the French and Swiss rudimental systems, however, this phrase is regarded as a roll made up of three strokes. The French word *ra* and the Swiss *Ruf* (both meaning *"roll"*) thus automatically indicate a different (and wider) distance between the notes (as opposed to the musical idea of a flam). Even older editions of the *All American Drummer* include passages that mention 3 str., although in the traditional first collection of rudiments (mentioned earlier in this book) there is no such thing as a *3-stroke roll* listed. Col. Hart, however, mentions a *3-roll* in his *New & Improved Instructor for the Drum* written in 1862. Anyhow, the density and distance between strokes on the *3-roll* would be very much comparable to how we structure a *5-stroke roll*. And there is evidence of a much "wider" and more "open" sounding style of drumming in the olden days as opposed to how rudimental drummers drum today. (*Author's note*: Even today in Basel drumming, our *5-stroke roll* is referred to as a *Fünfer Ruf* [*5-roll*], and a *7-stroke roll* as a *Siebener Ruf* [*7-roll*]. With that background, the combination RRL or LLR will automatically be a *Dreier Ruf* or *3-stroke roll*.) The word *drag* is probably not onomatopoeic but more likely relates to the process of dragging the stick across the drumhead to produce more than one note (see also *Encyclopedia of Percussion* by John Beck).

It is also very likely that the German word *Ruf* (pronounced like in the word *roof*) is the origin of the English word *ruff*. Older English sources sometimes even use the spellings *ruffe* or *roofe*. In a more traditional context the terms *ruff* and *drag* thus stand for the same combination of strokes. Slowly but surely the meaning of ruff has changed, however. When we speak of *ruffs* today, we usually mean a chain of single strokes (alternating sticking) of different length, e.g., the 4-stroke ruff would be RLRL or LRLR. Here is a little overview to give more clarification:

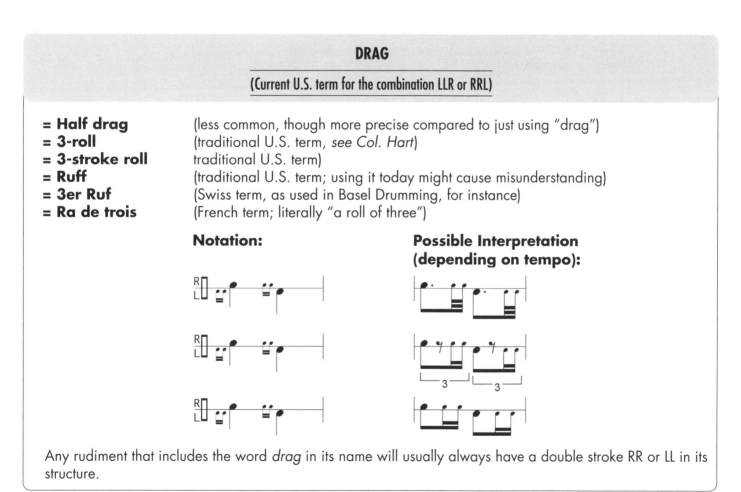

DRAG

(Current U.S. term for the combination LLR or RRL)

= **Half drag**	(less common, though more precise compared to just using "drag")
= **3-roll**	(traditional U.S. term, *see Col. Hart*)
= **3-stroke roll**	traditional U.S. term)
= **Ruff**	(traditional U.S. term; using it today might cause misunderstanding)
= **3er Ruf**	(Swiss term, as used in Basel Drumming, for instance)
= **Ra de trois**	(French term; literally "a roll of three")

Notation: **Possible Interpretation (depending on tempo):**

Any rudiment that includes the word *drag* in its name will usually always have a double stroke RR or LL in its structure.

For the sake of completeness it should be mentioned that a *drag* (as mentioned in the previous box) is not always a *single drag*. Thus the term *half drag* (as already used by Charles Ashworth) really does make sense. On the *single drag* (or *single drag tap*, which is the same pattern) one more stroke is added.

THREE BASIC "DRAG" RUDIMENTS | AN OVERVIEW

Half drag—sometimes just referred to as a *drag*
but not to be mixed up with the...

Single drag (tap)—the additional word *tap* is optional.
Related to the *Rigodon* in French and Swiss rudimental drumming.

Double drag (tap)—the additional word *tap* is optional. Related to the
Diane in the French tradition or the *Tagwachtstreich* in the Swiss tradition.

See
p. 75
Another related rudiment (whose name, however, is not related to the drag) would be the *lesson 25* (*see* →*appendix 1*). I like to consider a drag rudiment to be the shortest form of a *roll* rudiment—and not as an extra species of pattern. We could look at *roll* and *ruff* rudiments as a parallel to *drag* rudiments. Again, here's a short overview:

5-STROKE ROLL

(Current U.S. Term for the Combination LLRRL or RRLLR)

= Mother   (traditional U.S. term, *see Charles Ashworth*)
= 5-roll   (traditional U.S. term, *see Col. Hart*)
= 5er Ruf   (Swiss and German term, as used in Basel drumming for instance)
= Ra de cinq   (French term; literally "a roll of five")

See
pp. 73
In the traditional sense, *roll* rudiments only exist with uneven numbers of strokes played (though there are exceptions). Usually you start the pattern with the left hand, and the final stroke is an accent. See →*appendix 1* for more information.

SINGLE-STROKE FOUR

(Current U.S. Term for the Combination RLRL / LRLR)

= 4-stroke ruff (traditional term; less used for RLRL or LRLR)

See
pp. 74
In contemporary nomenclature, *ruff* rudiments describe chains of alternating single strokes and can be looked at as the offspring of the single-stroke roll. A 7-stroke ruff would thus be sticked RLRLRLR or LRLRLRL; a 3-stroke ruff would be RLR or LRL (usually not played with alternating sticking) and should not be confused with a *drag*. *Note*: Traditionally speaking, the *ruff* was meant to be RRL or LLR (see also →*rudiment no. 8* in *appendix 1*).

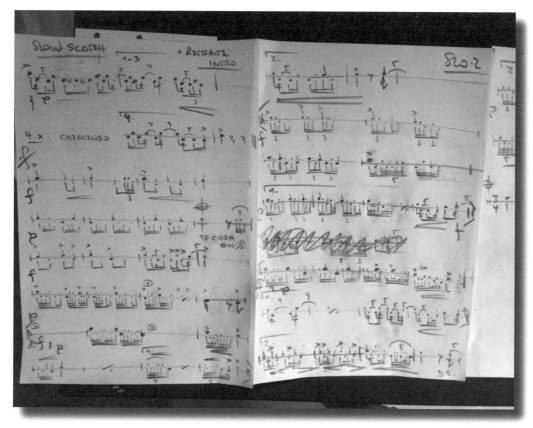

A first sketch of *Another Slow Scotch*.
Photo by Claus Hessler

𝕬𝖎𝖗 𝖉𝖊𝖘 𝕱𝖎𝖋𝖗𝖊𝖘 𝖔𝖚 𝕳𝖆𝖚𝖙𝖇𝖔𝖎𝖘

Anonymous Portrait of André Danican Philidor (appr. 1680)

See p. 9.

This musical piece first appeared in a collection called *Partitions de Plusieurs Marches* by André Danican Philidor (1652–1730), a court musician and composer by trade in the service of French King Louis XIV. He played the oboe, flute, and fife with musketeer units in the French army and composed and collected music ranging from simple instrumental compositions to operas, as well as military marches—you name it, he wrote it. This tune originates from a much older signal for the assembly of troops, as discussed in the earlier section about the 17th century. It is not known if the fife melody (most likely added at a later point) was composed by Philidor. The term *fifres ou houtbois* ("fife or oboe") suggests the choice of either fife or oboe and goes back to a reformation in military music at the end of the 17th century, when lead instruments changed from fifes to oboes. Fifes were definitely in use before then, but later were only found in Swiss units in the service of the French kings (we have already mentioned the *Cent Suisse* or →*Gardes du Corps Suisse*). In my notation of the original score I have made some minor changes in order to allow for better understanding of the music. The rhythmic information, however, remains unchanged. I also referenced a version of "Air des Fifres ou Hautbois" that I heard from the *Colonial Williamsburg Fifes and Drums* at PASIC 2011. I made some minor changes to the fife score, but nothing that would change the character of the piece in any drastic way. Although the original score does not display any real technical challenges, you should make sure that the majestic and graceful character of the piece is retained—creating a musical statement with very few notes can be a true art form as you will notice. With that in mind I think it is justifiable to work with dynamics to a certain degree, even though the chart itself does not state any dynamics. I know it is pure speculation, but I imagine it is very likely that the drummers who played this tune did the same in order to make it sound more musical and expressive. To imitate the sound of the big drums used around this time, I worked with extremely low tuning, which helped me think and play differently. I could understand the parallels between the fife and drum parts; the drums back up the fifes very actively, and do not just accompany the melody by simply marking a certain pulse or keeping time. Remarkably, the original score shows the meters changing from $\frac{2}{2}$ to $\frac{3}{2}$ and back. So, here it is:

Track 01: Demo Track 03: Play-Along Track 04: Play-Along (slow)

𝕬𝖎𝖗 𝖉𝖊𝖘 𝕱𝖎𝖋𝖗𝖊𝖘 𝖔𝖚 𝕳𝖆𝖚𝖙𝖇𝖔𝖎𝖘
Revised Notation of the Original Score

Play 4 x

rit.

I have used different strategies in my updated version of the piece. One of them is to connect, or "tie," relevant notes of the melody with rolls of different structure. In Basel drumming we sometimes hear of *Roulée* versions of drumming pieces that follow the same strategy. Many of these passages work with a basic structure of quintuplets; traditional American rudimental drumming, on the other hand, does not really have such a rhythmic background. The appendix includes a bunch of ideas and exercises to help you polish and fine-tune this concept. The 9-stroke rolls appearing in line four correspond well with exercise →*no. 5* of *appendix 2*, especially the first measure in these two following lines:

See
p. 80.

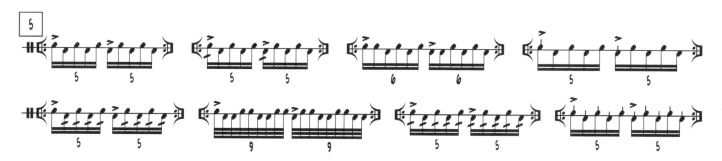

I would also recommend checking out *exercise nos. 18* and *20* of →*appendix 2* as well as *nos. 25* and *26* of → *appendix 1*. With this additional material you should be ready for:

See
p. 82/83

See
p. 78.

𝔄𝔦𝔯 𝔡𝔢𝔰 𝔉𝔦𝔣𝔯𝔢𝔰 𝔬𝔲 𝔥𝔞𝔲𝔱𝔟𝔬𝔦𝔰
"𝔯𝔬𝔲𝔩é𝔢"

Arranged by Claus Hessler

Track 02: Demo

Track 03: Play-Along

Track 04: Play-Along (slow)

To provide further assistance, here is a written-out version of the previous updated piece. Of course, there is a lot more music to read here, but on the other hand you'll notice exactly where the notes you play would really be located. As always, any written music is subject to personal interpretation.

𝕬𝖎𝖗 𝖉𝖊𝖘 𝕱𝖎𝖋𝖗𝖊𝖘 𝖔𝖚 𝕳𝖆𝖚𝖙𝖇𝖔𝖎𝖘 "Roulée"

Interpretation Guide

Track 02: Demo
Track 03: Play-Along
Track 04: Play-Along (slow)

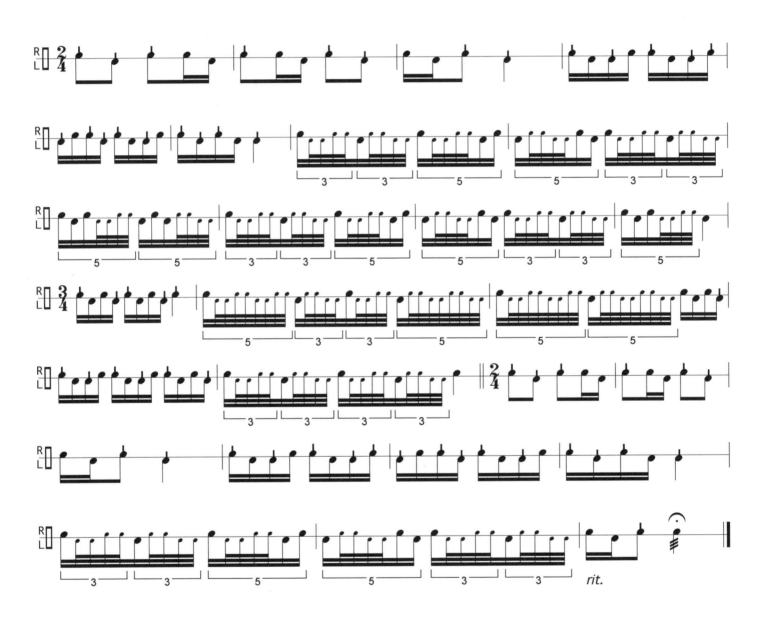

Depending on your own musical expression, it would also be possible to play more in unison with the fifes. (*Author's note*: Neither traditional American rudimental drumming nor Swiss drumming put any great emphasis on this.) The 5-stroke rolls, however, could still be "wider"; the following examples will give you some more ideas about how that could look. The corresponding measures of the interpretation guide are compared with further interpretation options:

Air des fifres ou hautbois "Roulée" | **Additional options for interpretation**

Left side: Passages taken from the interpretation guide   Right side: Further interpretation options

From this Baroque predecessor of fife and drum rudimental music, and with our diverse historical background knowledge, we can turn to the main focus of this book: the classic rudimental pieces taken from the "songbook" of the North American military tradition, but with strong European roots, as you will notice. Most of these pieces date from the late 18th and early 19th centuries. The updated versions I composed still relate to the original fife melody, but the drumming vocabulary uses many features taken from the Swiss, French, and modern American rudimental schools of drumming. In many cases I also used the element of so-called "collapsed" or "uncollapsed" rudiments. In my double DVD *Drumming Kairos* I go into more detail about this principle (which goes back to the late great Jim Chapin); in the chapter *Rudimental Approach* in my book *Open-Handed Playing Vol. 2: A Step Beyond* (published with Dom Famularo), you will also find a number of exercises that are similar to those in →appendix 2.

See pp. 79.

Shooting for the cover of *Camp Duty Update*. Our cat, Crumb, is assisting...
Photo by Claus Hessler

CHAPTER 2 | PIECES FROM THE U.S. CAMP & GARRISON DUTY

BACKGROUND OF THE CAMP & GARRISON DUTY

The *Camp & Garrison Duty* (or *Camp Duty* for short) describes a collection of tunes, marches, signals, etc., that any Army drummer of the 19th century had to master. The numerous beats relate to the different tasks and the daily routine that soldiers had to complete in the camp or garrison. The so-called *field music* (meaning drummers and fifers alike) would perform these calls and signals either at a given, specified time or to order. In keeping with the rest of the book I will only describe some of the more basic aspects. The daily routine in the military would, of course, begin with a ceremony to wake up the troops, known as the...

REVEILLE

At 06:00 am (sometimes even earlier) drummers and fifers gather and perform a defined collection of pieces. This routine evolved over the years; by the middle of the 19th century it looked like this:

- No. 1: *The Three Camps* (also known as *Points of War*)
- No. 2: *The Slow Scotch*
- No. 3: *The Austrian*
- No. 4: *Dawning of the Day* (an optional part of the routine according to Bruce & Emmett)
- No. 5: *The Hessian*
- No. 6: *Dusky Night* (also optional according to Bruce & Emmett an optional part, could be omitted)
- No. 7: *The Prussian*
- No. 8: *The Dutch*
- No. 9: *The Quick Scotch*
- and again a part of the *Three Camps* for the ending.

Further parts of the reveille included:

DRUMMER'S CALL

Using this signal the drummer on duty (or the drum major) called the other drummers to service. This signal would thus also precede the *Three Camps*; as a further option there was was a "band call," which would automatically include the fifers too. It was played by the drummer of the guard at the guard house.

PIONEER'S CALL OR FATIGUE

This was played 15 minutes after the *reveille* and was the signal for special groups of workers to clean and clear up the parade ground, etc. At the same time it was the order for so-called *disorderly women* to leave the camp...

ASSEMBLY

This was the signal for troops to assemble by company and to proceed (e.g., to drill or parade).

SURGEON'S CALL

This was played one hour before the *Breakfast Call*, sometimes also at different times if so ordered. Sick or injured soldiers fit for transport were to be transferred to the military hospital by the non-commissioned officer in charge.

BREAKFAST CALL (PEAS UPON A TRENCHER)

This was the signal for breakfast and was usually played at 7 a.m. in case there was no other order. Fifteen minutes beforehand the drummer on duty played the *Drummer's Call* or the *Band Call* to call the *field music*.

DINNER CALL (ROASTBEEF)

This was the signal for lunch and was usually played at 12 noon. Fifteen minutes beforehand the signal was preannounced by the *Drummer's Call*. (*Author's note*: The term "dinner" in this case refers to the midday meal.) The original text in Bruce & Emmett's *The Drummers' and Fifers' Guide* clearly states: "Dinner Call is the signal for dinner, and is usually beat at 12 o'clock.")

RETREAT

Usually played at sunset, all retreats began and ended with the *Three Cheers*—a typical short combination of rolls and crescendos/decrescendos at the end. In bad weather conditions a short form was used, the so-called *Quick Retreat*.

TATTOO—EVENING DUTY

Usually played at 9 p.m., after which no soldier or member of the field music should be outside of his tent or quarters. Fifteen minutes after that the drummer on duty played a final signal to extinguish lights.

The full list of calls and corresponding regulations is, of course, somewhat longer and includes any important matter that had to be taken care of in the daily routine of the Army:

calling soldiers to religious service (the *Church Call*);
announcing negotiations with the enemy (the *Parley*);
the *Funeral March*;
the *Rogues March*, which was played to drum "unworthy" soldiers out of service;
loading muskets;
fire;
the *Wood Call*;
the *Water Call*;
fixing bayonets or taking them down, etc.

Just about anything in the daily routine was announced and ordered through the corresponding calls of field drums and fifes. This book will teach you some of them, but we will focus on those that have the character of a recognizable musical piece and not just the short signals made up of a one- or two-bar phrase.

A rare snapshot of Claus with field drum, sling, and traditional grip—
taken at the shooting of the DVD *Drumming Kairos*.
Photo by Florian Alexandru-Zorn

𝕿𝖍𝖊 𝕿𝖍𝖗𝖊𝖊 𝕮𝖆𝖒𝖕𝖘 𝖔𝖗 𝕻𝖔𝖎𝖓𝖙𝖘 𝖔𝖋 𝖂𝖆𝖗

HISTORY AND BACKGROUND

The Three Camps represented the first musical event in the daily routine of the U.S. Army; it was the first tune in the *Camp and Garrison Duty* and was played at sunrise. The drummer and fifer on duty would play a signal (the *Drummer's Call*) for the other members of the field music and call them to service. As soon as all the field musicians had gathered, they would play the *Three Camps* as the wake-up call for the troops. In Basel drumming we have the parallel of the so-called *Tagwacht*, whereas in the French tradition the wake-up call was referred to as the *Diane*. The Swiss *Tagwacht* and the *Diane* appear to be quite similar in structure, whereas the *Three Camps* are somewhat different with regard to the patterns and rhythms used.

The *Three Camps* or *Points of War* appear in literally all the drum methods of the 19th century and cannot be attributed to a certain composer. It appears in Ashworth's *New, Useful and Complete System of Drum Beating* (1812), and later in *The Drummers' and Fifers' Guide*, the *Moeller Book*, as well as Charley Wilcoxon's *Modern Rudimental Swing Solos*, to mention just a few. The tune itself is not that demanding. However, its notation appears to be somewhat inconvenient in many cases; even skilled sight-readers will most likely be stretched to their limits, making misinterpretation easy to occur. Since it seems unlikely that you can play the piece in the intended way after having studied the books mentioned, I have chosen to notate the piece in $\frac{6}{8}$ time. This turns out to be a little clearer, as it lets you leave out the triplet brackets.

Bruce & Emmett *The Drummers' and Fifers' Guide* (around 1865) | Reprint available at http://www.beafifer.com

The alternate title "Points of War" most likely goes back to a British term used in the mid 17th century, describing the necessary signal to maneuver military units ("charge," "troop," "retreat," etc.). In Levi Lovering's book we also hear of a musical imitation of a battle, while Charles Ashworth still mentions the *Points of War* (especially the *First Camp*) as a special salute for a governor or the president.

When comparing the different versions of Lovering, Col. Hart, Bruce & Emmett, etc., there are in fact a number of differences ranging from variations of the fife melody to different structures of the rolls used. In my notation of the original score I chose the one that turned out to be a standard version by the end of the 19th century. The list of rudiments used is not that overwhelming: 5-stroke rolls, 11-stroke rolls, later 10-stroke rolls, and one single drag tap at the very end. The structure of the last bar also differs in certain books; sometimes it is just a copy of the second-to-last bar (two 5-stroke rolls, no single drag), while at other times the accents are different (accents on beats 1 and 4, otherwise as shown here). Traditionally, each tune of the reveille ends with a long roll in $\frac{2}{4}$ time using sixteenth-note subdivisions, which I have also added here. As mentioned earlier, the tune is not really that complex, but it still needs to be performed in a musical and tasteful way. The following example describes the structure of the rolls; for the 10-stroke roll appearing later in the piece, you just replace the double stroke on beat 6 in measures 2 and 4 with an accented single stroke.

𝕿𝖍𝖗𝖊𝖊 𝕮𝖆𝖒𝖕𝖘 | 5-stroke roll and 11-stroke roll in $\frac{6}{8}$ time

Bars 1 and 2: Usual notation   Bars 3 and 4: Execution in detail

Three Camps · Original Score

Traditional | Revised Notation

Track 05:
Demo

Track 07:
Play-Along

Track 08:
Play-Along (slow)

Open roll based on 16th notes -

The dotted quarter notes in $\frac{6}{8}$ time correspond with the quarter notes in $\frac{2}{4}$ time.

The following updated version offers more variations with regard to how you could structure single and double strokes in a 5-stroke roll structure; it still follows the same flute melody. One of the challenges might also be the septuplet phrase in *line 7, second measure*. The structure can be seen as an *uncollapsed* final stroke of seven (taken from the Swiss/Basel tradition of drumming). Check out *exercise no. 20* in →*appendix 2!*

See
p. 83.

Another Three Camps

Arranged by Claus Hessler

Open roll based on sixteenth notes -
The dotted quarter notes in $\frac{6}{8}$ time correspond with the quarter notes in $\frac{2}{4}$ time.

𝔅𝔯𝔢𝔞𝔨𝔣𝔞𝔰𝔱 𝔠𝔞𝔩𝔩
"𝔓𝔢𝔞𝔰 𝔘𝔭𝔬𝔫 𝔞 𝔗𝔯𝔢𝔫𝔠𝔥𝔢𝔯"

HISTORY AND BACKGROUND

Like many pieces from the Camp Duty of the U.S. Army, the *Breakfast Call* evolved from a number of diverse sources. As with the *Dinner Call*, the original part for field drums is technically not that hard to play. And once again this piece is notated rather cryptically in different books and drum manuals. Since the tune is not that demanding technically, the notation itself is difficult to decode at times. The melody of the *Breakfast Call* is actually an Irish folk song by the name of *Peas Upon a Trencher*. The piece became popular by reason of the connection with a poem (published in 1817) by Irish writer Thomas Moore (1780–1852).

Moore was raised in a Catholic middle-class home and had an early affinity for writing, reportedly first publishing works in Dublin around 1790 (at the age of ten). His family was also sympathetic to the ideals of the American and French Revolutions and the promise of a better quality of life for the lower classes. Between 1808 and 1834 Moore published a collection of songs for voice and piano in ten volumes, called *The Irish Melodies*, in which he set 124 of his poems to traditional Irish melodies. In the Camp Duty, both the titles *Peas Upon a Trencher* and *Breakfast Call* are linked to the tune. "The Time I've Lost in Wooing." Here's the first verse of the poem:

IRISH MELODIES
BY
THOMAS MOORE

LONDON
LONGMAN, GREEN, LONGMAN, ROBERTS, & GREEN
1865

Thomas Moore, *The Irish Melodies*
(Edition from 1865)

"The time I've lost in wooing, in watching and pursuing,

The light that lies in woman's eyes has been my heart's undoing.

Tho' wisdom oft has sought me, I spurned the lore she taught me

My only books were woman's looks and folly's all they taught me!"

The piece includes three basic patterns: the 7-stroke roll, the single drag tap, and the 5-stroke roll. In Basel drumming, the single drag tap is usually referred to as the *Rigodon* (*see also the overview of →rudiments at the end of this book*). Though the notation used in the original score mostly uses $\frac{2}{4}$ time, the whole piece is constantly played in a triplet-like feel. As the relation between *pulse* and the patterns used can be shown better in a $\frac{6}{8}$ context, I went for a corresponding update. The dotted 16th notes and 32nd notes in the original score also make the piece look much more difficult than it really is. Using this style of notation for the single drag tap creates similar challenges for some Wilcoxon solos (for instance *nos. 132 or 133*). The phrase seems out of context compared with the other rudiments used, and usually slows down the tempo for the whole piece, which is a real pity.

↓ See ↓ pp. 79.

The following box shows first how the cornerstones of the *Breakfast Call* are traditionally notated (according to Moeller or Bruce & Emmett) and then how they would be interpreted:

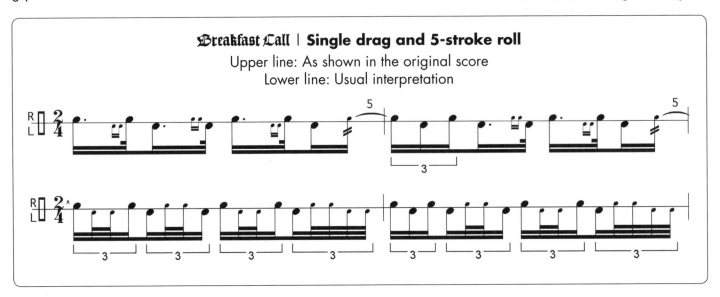

Just like the *Dinner Call* and most other pieces of the Camp Duty, the *Breakfast Call* does not have any real dynamic design as such, but the two accents in the third line are relevant to the melody of the fifes. *Remember*: Rimshots on traditional rudimental pieces are primarily a "no go." The drags are on beats 2 and 5 and should not be squeezed too tightly towards the following note:

Breakfast Call
"Peas Upon a Trencher"
Traditional | Revised Notation

The updated version offers some room for debate with regards to certain variations of the sticking in different rhythms. Again you'll find a whole range of unusual rhythmic vocabulary and an interesting version of a roll in septuplets.

Another Breakfast Call
(Too Many Peas Upon a Trencher)

Arranged by Claus Hessler

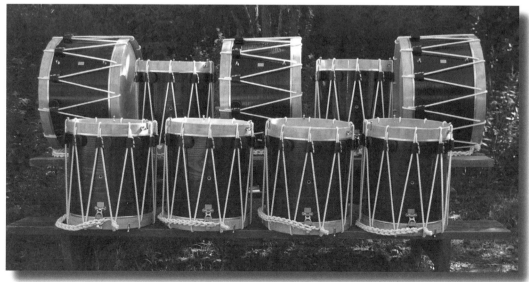

Traditional set of bass drums, tenor drums, and field drums
Picture courtesy of Patsy Ellis, Cooperman Rope Tension Drums

𝕯𝖎𝖓𝖓𝖊𝖗 𝕮𝖆𝖑𝖑: "𝕿𝖍𝖊 𝕽𝖔𝖆𝖘𝖙𝖇𝖊𝖊𝖋 𝖔𝖋 𝕺𝖑𝖉 𝕰𝖓𝖌𝖑𝖆𝖓𝖉"

HISTORY AND BACKGROUND

Here's another standard taken from the Camp Duty—the *Dinner Call*, also known as *Roast Beef* or *Roastbeef of Old England*. As already mentioned, the piece itself was intended to call the soldiers to the midday meal and was usually beaten at 12 noon.

See ⬇
p. 38.
The notation and structure of this call changed quite a bit through the years. *The Revolutionary War Drill Manual* still refers to the term *Roast Beef* and not the *Dinner Call*, though both terms refer to the same tune or signal. Some commands and the corresponding beat of the drums are described verbally in Steuben's regulations, using terminology such as *flam, drag,* or *poing stroke,* but you'll search in vain for written music. Charles Ashworth also refers to just *Roast Beef,* without mentioning the *Dinner Call.* With Ashworth we find some triplet structures, but not in all the places where they will appear later (*see the →original score on page 38*). We can only speculate if people liked the triplet additions to such a degree that they were then increasingly added to the piece. While Ashworth denotes no 9-stroke rolls, he does include 7-stroke rolls and 5-stroke rolls. The Samuel Potter manual seems to be one of the first books where you really find the term *Dinner Call* along with *The Roast Beef of Old England.* Again, this is further evidence for the fact that this piece obviously has British rather than American roots (*Author's note*: Samuel Potter and Charles Ashworth were both British). Potter already shows the double drag taps using rhythms in dotted eighth notes, but the additional 9-stroke roll is missing. Bruce & Emmett show the rolls and the triplets, but the double drags are notated in a straight eighth-note rhythm—not the typical dotted notes. The notation I have used here is mostly based on the common form as it is found around the end of the 19th century. As most of the manuals for fife and drums around this time include the Camp Duty, a lot of matching information can be found. An interesting variation can be found in the British *Drum and Flute Duty* from 1887, which indicates "Swiss-like" reveille (Tagwacht) patterns; also, the *Dinner Call* does not start with the typical 7-stroke roll but an "open flam" (where both notes are accented).

Sanford Moeller's *The Art of Snare Drumming* shows a version that leaves us guessing about the structure of the rolls. Again we find a very careful and detailed notation—but only insiders who already know the piece would be able to understand what Moeller really meant. The following example shows the typical structure of the *Dinner Call* and its interpretation:

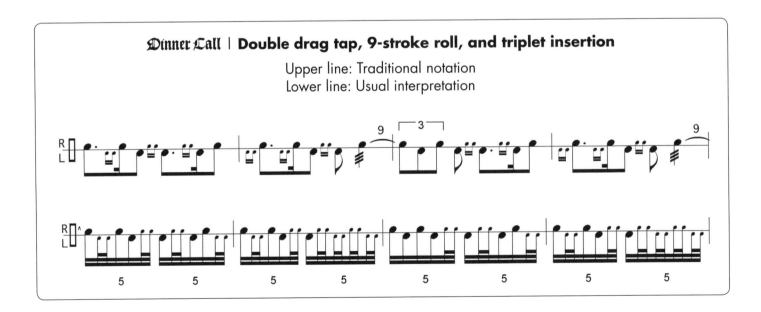

𝕯𝖎𝖓𝖓𝖊𝖗 𝕮𝖆𝖑𝖑 | Double drag tap, 9-stroke roll, and triplet insertion

Upper line: Traditional notation
Lower line: Usual interpretation

A lot of comparable structures can be found in the Swiss *Tagwacht* as well as in the French tradition of rudimental drumming. The French used patterns known as *Diane*, also describing a combination of a double drag tap and a 9-stroke roll. The following box (using "Berger" notation) clearly outlines the parallels between the *Dinner Call* and a *Tagwacht* as played in Swiss/Basel drumming:

Excerpt from the Badac Tagwacht (Berger notation):

Image *Tagwacht*: Claus Hessler

The example above also showcases the conceptual advantage of the "Berger notation style." The tiresome discussion about when exactly the 9-stroke roll has to start is thus made superfluous. Still the single note played with the left hand on beat 2 (the small note whose flags extend into the quarter-note stem) is compulsory— immediately after that the 9-stroke roll begins. Thus, the roll will literally be squeezed between two notes.

The system using quintuplets is surprisingly close to the musical reality and works nicely to explain the structure of the pattern. The following example describes another challenge of the piece:

Dinner Call | Double drag tap and 9-stroke roll

Upper line: Traditional notation
Lower line: Interpretation

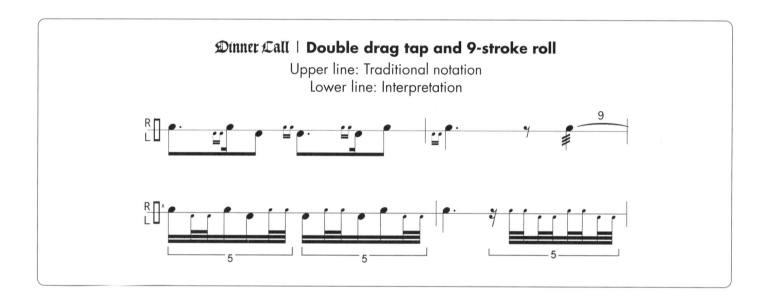

When working on the updated version *Another Dinner Call* I would recommend the following additional exercises from the →*appendices* for further practice:

See pp. 73.

See pp. 79.

APPENDIX 1	APPENDIX 2
No. 10: Double drag tap or single reveille stroke	No. 22
No. 11: Reversed reveille stroke	No. 24
No. 21: 9-stroke roll	No. 1/No. 5
No. 25: Complete final stroke of seven	No. 20
No. 26: Reversed, complete final stroke of seven	No. 18
No. 27: Reveille stroke, 3-stroke roll combination	No. 25

See ↓
p. 79. ▼
In →*appendix 2* a variety of accent studies based on the rhythmic grid of quintuplets are shaped in different ways using flams, double strokes, and the idea of collapsed and uncollapsed rudiments. Working on these patterns continuously will definitely improve your understanding and sense of orientation in unusual rhythmic layers. Here is the original score of the *Dinner Call:*

Track 13:
Demo

Track 15:
Play-Along

Track 16:
Play-Along (slow)

𝕯inner 𝕮all ⁄ 𝕺riginal 𝕾core
"𝕿he 𝕽oastbeef of 𝕺ld 𝕰ngland"

Traditional

Rope tension field drum by Eli Brown & Son
with typical tacking pattern from 1842.
Picture courtesy of Patsy Ellis, Cooperman Rope Tension Drums.

Another Dinner Call

Arranged by Claus Hessler

As an additional help here's another guide for interpretation, giving you more detailed information about the patterns and their structure. Of course, this means reading more—but this way you get a very clear statement regarding placement of drags and rolls:

Another Dinner Call

Interpretation Guide

𝕯𝖚𝖘𝖐𝖞 𝕹𝖎𝖌𝖍𝖙

HISTORY AND BACKGROUND

There is a lot of conflicting information about when *Dusky Night*—also known as *Dusky Night Rides Down the Sky*—was first released or published. The melody was played throughout the 18th century using a number of different titles; one of the better-known references is the manuscript of George Bush, a Captain of the Continental Army during the War of Independence. (It would be interesting to know if there's a link to the family of U.S. Presidents!)

You can also find a version for fifes and drums in *The Drummers' and Fifers' Guide* by George Bruce and Daniel Emmett. They mention that this tune was really only added for reasons of tradition—around the time of Bruce and Emmett the tune wasn't a firm part of the *Camp Duty* anymore (just like *Dawning of the Day*, for example). Sanford Moeller also included a version of *Dusky Night* in his *The Art of Snare Drumming*, obviously referring to the Bruce & Emmett version. It is also very likely that a recorded performance of the Eastman Wind Ensemble with Frederick Fennell (and the suggestive title *Spirit of '76*) is responsible for the deviation from the typical combination of the 9-stroke roll and the double drag tap. For that reason I decided to include two different "original versions" in this book.

The following box shows how the tune is interpreted in the Fennell recording, following the notation of Moeller and Bruce & Emmett. The eighth notes sound very "straight" and thus completely unlike the way they are usually played on a piece like the *Dinner Call*, for instance. On Fennel's version the 9-stroke roll only really starts on beat 5 (and not before as you might think). This execution definitely adds a hardness to the patterns played; the flowing and rolling character of the *Dinner Call* is now gone, even though the structures of the phrases are very similar.

Frederick Fennell and members of the Eastman Wind Ensemble:
The Spirit of '76 and Ruffles and Flourishes
Mercury Living Presence. item-#: 434 386-2

𝕯𝖚𝖘𝖐𝖞 𝕹𝖎𝖌𝖍𝖙 | Alternative double drag tap and 9-stroke roll

Bars 1 and 2: Notation based on Sanford Moeller and Bruce & Emmett
Bars 3 and 4: Corresponding interpretation with Frederick Fennell's Eastman Wind Ensemble

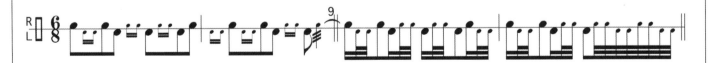

Dusky Night — Original Score No. 1

Traditional
Notation based on The Art of Snare Drumming (Sanford Moeller)
and The Drummers' & Fifers' Guide (Bruce & Emmett)

Track 17:
Demo

Track 20:
Play-Along

Track 21:
Play-Along (slow)

Personally I think that it is rather likely that the tune was played as shown in version no. 2. When you compare the *Dinner Call* and *Dusky Night* as whole pieces you'll discover astonishing parallels, if not complete conformity. I guess this might be a reason why the tune was removed from the *Camp Duty*. All in all, this version has a more flowing and elegant tone though this is to a certain degree only in the eye (or better the ear) of the beholder.

Dusky Night | 9-stroke roll, 7-stroke roll, triplet insertion, and double drag tap

Bars 1/2 and 5/6: A usual form of notation
Bars 3/4 and 7/8: Corresponding interpretation

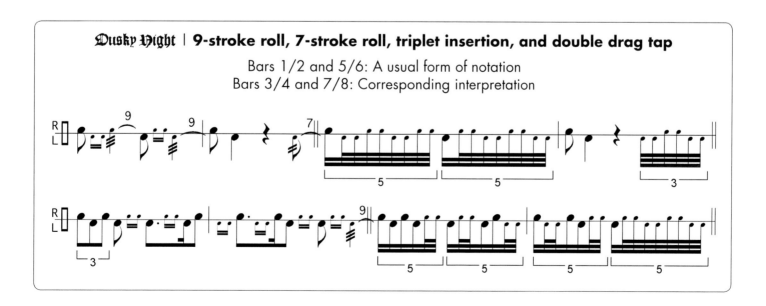

𝕯𝖚𝖘𝖐𝖞 𝕹𝖎𝖌𝖍𝖙 ~ 𝕺𝖗𝖎𝖌𝖎𝖓𝖆𝖑 𝕾𝖈𝖔𝖗𝖊 𝕹𝖔. 2

Traditional
Alternative Interpretation

Track 18:
Demo

Track 20:
Play-Along

Track 21:
Play-Along (slow)

Field drum built by Sanford Moeller for the Mount Vernon Field Music; around 1940.
Picture courtesy of Patsy Ellis, Cooperman Rope Tension Drums

Another Dusky Night

Arranged by Claus Hessler

Track 19: Demo
Track 20: Play-Along
Track 21: Play-Along (slow)

Picture taken during the shooting of *Drumming Kairos* playing *Another Three Camps*.
Picture courtesy of Florian Alexandru-Zorn

The Slow Scotch

HISTORY AND BACKGROUND

Another component of the *Camp Duty*, *The Slow Scotch* was the second tune of the reveille after *The Three Camps*. The tune is also one of the few pieces in the *Camp Duty* in which the dynamic structure is a typical, characteristic aspect. The main challenge is to maintain the majestic character of the tune, allowing for enough gravity as you perform it. The original score of *The Slow Scotch* does not include any tricky or complex patterns. The tempo itself is rather on the slow side and so provides for a manageable stock of phrases. As the tempo allows I play the drags relatively close on the accompanying CD; a number of sources back up this approach.

See
p. 77. Despite the slow tempo of the tune, the 7-stroke rolls are already dense enough to present a certain amount of intricacy. The following box explains the triplet-like structure of the rolls in $\frac{2}{4}$ time (see also rudiment →*no. 20* in *appendix no. 1*):

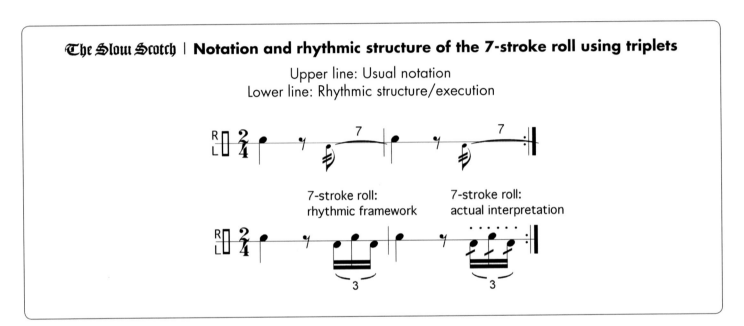

The Slow Scotch | Notation and rhythmic structure of the 7-stroke roll using triplets

Upper line: Usual notation
Lower line: Rhythmic structure/execution

7-stroke roll:
rhythmic framework

7-stroke roll:
actual interpretation

As we have already heard, the names of many pieces in the Camp Duty offer a hint to a country or region linked to them, such as *The Slow Scotch*, *The Hessian*, or *The Dutch* to name a few. Unfortunately it is not always possible to collect reliable information about the origin of the flute melodies and drumming and their See
pp. 40. geographical background. But we do know that certain nations could be identified by their typical marches and beats (as discussed in the →*preceding chapter*). British references from the 16th and 17th centuries also suggest that knowledge of foreign marches and signals must also have been a special qualification for drummers of this era.

There is also evidence that tunes and drum beats were exported to other fighting nations/units and from army to army—in some cases even from friend to foe or vice versa, as we will hear later. The more seasoned drummers are thus bound to have had knowledge about the tunes and drum beats of other units or armies. The family relations between European monarchs was reason enough for brotherhood in arms. Hessian soldiers (from the more southern part of Germany) were lent to the British in order to fight against the American mavericks in the *War of Independence*, for instance. It is also likely that some Prussian influence was imported to the U.S. by the input of Friedrich von Steuben (who acted as a kind of hired "coach" for the U.S. Army). Presumably these two examples form the background for the tunes known as *The Hessian* or *The Prussian*. Here now is the original score of *The Slow Scotch*:

The Slow Scotch – Original

Traditional

Track 22: Demo
Track 23: Play-Along
Track 24: Play-Along (slow)

In the following updated version I have also added both an intro and an outro in the style of a Swiss *retraite*. Sometimes the preludes of these pieces do not even have a clearly assigned time or measure; in certain cases they are really a demanding mixture of connected rolls and Swiss "final strokes" requiring remarkable technical and rhythmical skills. In this case I chose $\frac{3}{4}$ for the intro—which is again typical for traditional American retreats. Interestingly enough these also have a characteristic intro, the so-called *Three Cheers*, meaning a combination of rolls in a four-bar phrase using crescendos.

Track 25:
Demo

Track 26:
Play-Along

Track 27:
Play-Along (slow)

Another Slow Scotch

Arranged by Claus Hessler

"Retraite" Style Intro

Again here's an interpretation guide without abbreviated notation for the rolls. This might be helpful especially for the intro and outro sections of the tune. The additional exercises in →*appendix 2* are highly recommended. For better legibility I also show softer notes with a smaller notehead. When listening to the recorded performance and comparing sound and notation you should get a pretty good idea of how these two relate to each other.

 See pp. 79.

Track 25:
Demo

Track 26:
Play-Along

Track 27:
Play-Along (slow)

Another Slow Scotch

Interpretation Guide

"Retraite" Style Intro

CHAPTER 3 | TRADITIONAL "QUICKSTEPS" AND RUDIMENTAL CLASSICS

CONCERNING THE CHOICE AND ORIGIN OF TUNES

Besides the tunes included in the *Camp Duty* and the signals and drum beats used to communicate military orders, there is also an extensive collection of tunes that were spread in the military periphery and did not have a true function in the organization of the U.S. Army. People usually refer to so-called *quicksteps*, which found their way into the military via different routes. The cultural melting pot of influences from Ireland, Germany, Great Britain, or the Netherlands also added to the variety of the musical repertoire.

When selecting the tunes for this book I mostly stuck to the better-known representatives of this musical genre—some of the pieces will certainly sound familiar although you might not know all of them by name. Some of the tunes also have an interesting historical background, and we can also gain a more complete picture if we consider the corresponding spirit of the age.

We should also not forget that military music has always been much more than just a vehicle to convey orders or to instill fear into the enemy. Music also had a therapeutic function in helping the soldiers to regain their strength, to build morale, and to escape the everyday ordinary horror of war (for a while at least). We will start this next chapter with an all-time classic of rudimental drumming, the *Downfall of Paris*.

MILITARY DRUM BEATS

FOR SCHOOL AND DRUM CORPS

George Lawrence Stone

Book | ISBN: 978-1-892764-03-4

The Downfall of Paris

HISTORY AND BACKGROUND

The Downfall of Paris really is one of the most widespread and well-known rudimental pieces of all time. During the times of the *Civil War* the tune was employed as a so-called *tattoo* and was played in addition to the signals used to announce the end of the daily routine in the military, including indicating that (alcoholic) beverages would not be on tap anymore. The word *tattoo* itself possibly goes back to the Dutch phrase *taptoe* (tap closed), referring to when the officer on duty would sweep across the tap and close it. The German word *Zapfenstreich* (also still in use today) has the same original meaning. Besides the charts for fifes and drums, Sanford Moeller also added a statement about the *The Downfall of Paris* in his book as follows:

> "The 'Downfall of Paris' is one of the most ancient and perhaps the most famous of beats. It has always been the pride of the schooled drummers, not only to play it so it sounded correct but also to beat it in the prescribed way. When drummers from different parts of the country get together and drum such beats as this with perfect uniformity they prove themselves worthy brethren. The author finds, in his 15.000 mile trip around the U.S. in 1925, that there are hundreds of drummers with this accomplishment, and when they meet it is the beginning of a lifelong friendship."

Of course, a fair amount of pathos can be read between the lines, but Moeller's words only confirm that drummers must have always been a special breed of musicians with a sense of brotherhood towards each other. The quoted paragraph may provide us with a better understanding of how Moeller gained his legendary insight into certain techniques used by Army veterans. As we all know, the inspiration for the *Moeller Technique* came from watching these old men play tunes that they all remembered from their service in the Army. *The Downfall of Paris* was undoubtedly one of them. Comparing how people performed certain passages must have been a valuable source of information when it came to creating his technical system.

The name of the tune itself goes back to the invasion of allied troops in Paris in March 1815, shortly before the defeat of Napoleon at Waterloo in June of the same year. The melody of the song itself was already very common at this point, though under different names. One of the better-known tunes using that same theme was *Ça Ira* (translation: *it will work out somehow*), composed by M. Becourt, who is said to have been a drummer at a French concert hall. It is safe to say he will have had no idea about how his piece would go on to be used. His composition must have been a well-known *Cotillion*, a ballroom dance during the late 18th and early 19th centuries. (This kind of contradance also influenced the evolution of the *Danzon* in Cuba, by the way.) The title *Ça Ira* is said to have been influenced by a quote of Benjamin Franklin (1706–1790), "it will succeed"— Franklin wanted to express his optimism about the outcome of the revolution. General Lafayette liked that so much that he forwarded the statement to a well-known singer Ladré who finally made *Ça Ira* popular.

There are a number of different stories relating to the lyrics, too. At the time of the *French Revolution* between 1789 and 1799 the song was used to challenge the aristocrats in France, with the lyrics charging something to the effect that the aristocrats should all be hanged on a lamp post. In that regard the song was often heard during armed conflicts and executions of upper-class citizens.

The emigrants traveling to the New World would, of course, take the song and theme with them and spread it in the colonies using different titles again (for instance *Mississippi Sawyer*). Likewise there are records that point to the use of this theme in France and England. Again it is interesting to note that the song is not of American origin.

When we look at the stickings used in the original version of the tune we also find conflicting information among the different sources (Bruce & Emmett show no sticking at all, in fact). Again I tried to find a compromise by mixing versions from Sanford Moeller's *The Art of Snare Drumming* and J. Burns Moore's *Art of Drumming*. Whenever I have found conformity I have stuck with that sticking; in other places I have gone for what seems more realistic or practical. Especially the very first bar of the tune, which is often shown as it is in the example below:

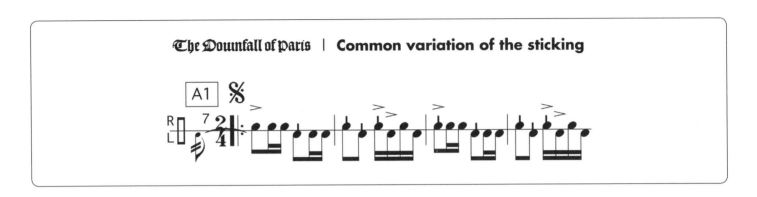

Moeller particularly emphasizes the correctness of the sticking of the tune in his publication, so ultimately I have decided to go with this less common version—and not the more frequently used one in the box above.

The 15-stroke roll in the B part of *The Downfall of Paris* might also need some extra explanation. On the CD for this book I have decided to use the more modern interpretation based on 16th notes, starting on beat 1e—not 1+. If you prefer a more traditional interpretation you might instead start the roll on the count of 1+, but you should note that the seven double strokes then get rather squeezed into the space before the next count of 1. In very traditional or ancient interpretations you can get away with playing the stroke notated on beat 1 a touch late. Allowing for a quintuplet-based rhythmic grid can also help to give the roll a more musical and forward-pressing sound, building to a climax on beat 1. A slight crescendo might even be welcome. Check out the box below:

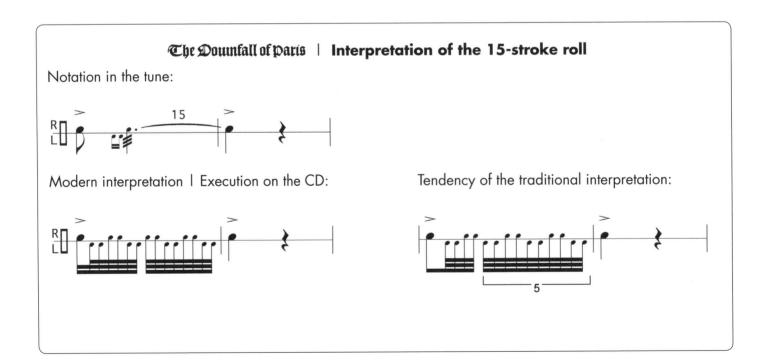

The Downfall of Paris – Original Score

Traditional

Stickings based on the versions of Sanford Moeller and J. Burns Moore

Track 28: Demo

Track 30: Play-Along

Track 31: Play-Along (slow)

The modern version does not hold too many rhythmical traps, though we do have to deal with a decent amount of flams. One of the interesting passages is the first three bars in the C part: Though the sticking remains unchanged, the distances between the notes are significantly altered. This is a good example of the influence of Chapin's *collapsed rudiments* as seen in this book. The flam on beat 1 is left out when doing the *D.S. jump* (also see the →*additional note marked by the **). The quintuplet-based phrases at the end of the tune shouldn't be too much of a problem by now, though the 5-stroke rolls at the very end might give you some challenges due to the density of strokes. And now enjoy!

See p. 54.

Another Downfall

Arranged by Claus Hessler

Track 29:
Demo

Track 30:
Play-Along

Track 31:
Play-Along (slow)

* The flam on the count of '1' in A1 is left out when doing the *D.S. jump.*

𝕲𝖆𝖗𝖗𝖞𝖔𝖜𝖊𝖓

HISTORY AND BACKGROUND

We have already seen from pieces like the *Dinner Call* or *The Downfall of Paris* that certain tunes have had a long history and thus were played in different environments over time. The *Garryowen*, whose Irish origins can be traced back to the 17th century, is no different.

The *Garryowen* seems to be one of the best-known musical themes of Ireland. The name itself is of Gaelic origin (originally *Garrai Eoin*) and refers to what is now a suburb of Limerick in the southern part of the island. One of the first military units to adopt the song was *The 5th Royal Irish Dragoons* for whom it became a kind of trademark, regimental tune. Disturbances and insubordination connected with the *Irish Rebellion* of 1798 (including alleged treachery) caused the relocation of the unit to England; ultimately the Dragoons then were disbanded by direct order of the British King in April 1799. Some of the soldiers emigrated to the United States, and went on to serve in the U.S. Army—and, of course, they also brought the song *Garryowen* with them. In later years, the 7th U.S. Cavalry adopted the tune. The story goes that Irishmen would sing this song under the influence of alcoholic refreshments, and General Custer liked it so much that he made it the regimental song, with the name *Garryowen* even appearing in the signs of this famous company. Besides these two regiments, *Garryowen* became the signature tune for several other military units, often also using different lyrics and variations of the theme itself. The song is now one of the most widespread tunes in the genre of military songs in the U.S.

In Basel, Switzerland, the theme also became part of a traditional march played for the *Fasnacht*, the so-called *Arabi*. The tune *Arabi* is also noteworthy since it is in fact not a medley of Swiss compositions and traditional melodies at all, but rather a compilation of English and Irish tunes. The first two verses are recognizable as the *British Grenadiers*, verses three and four are the *Garryowen*, while verses five and six are *The Girl I Left Behind*—which apparently was often played when military units left the garrison or town they had been staying in for a certain while. Using the indirect route via Basel, the theme of the *Garryowen* also made it into an orchestral piece, the so-called *Geigy Concert* of Swiss composer Rolf Liebermann. The intention of this composition was also to display a range of melodies connected with the town of Basel—and, of course, the *Arabi* and several solo parts featuring Basel drumming could not be left out of it.

By virtue of the many different versions and the broad stretch of time that this theme has been in use, it is very hard to substantiate today if there ever was such a thing as a historically definitive drum beat for this piece and, if so, who was responsible for it. It is worth bearing in mind that one or two standardized drum beats were in use for a string of songs, which would make sense in a certain way since tunes of similar form and rhythm could be accompanied by a consistent drumming part. This explains obvious similarities in the drum beats of certain tunes (e.g., *Dusky Night* →*Dinner Call* or *Dixie* →*British Grenadiers*). In order to make the following traditional version a little more interesting, I added an (almost) traditional intro and a so-called *roll off*. It was very common that, especially for the march, the drums would at times play alone, without the fifes. After calling the next tune, the *roll off* would be played (meaning the four-bar phrase in line three) and after that the actual tune would commence.

Garryowen – Original Score

Traditional

When modulating from $\frac{6}{8}$ to $\frac{2}{4}$ and back, the rhythmic pulse remains unchanged. The dotted quarter notes in $\frac{6}{8}$ time match the quarter notes in $\frac{2}{4}$ time.

D.S. al Coda senza rep.

Fine

In the updated version we find several more modern phrases and sticking instructions; the notation for the sound file should give a clear idea about the desired musical result. Still, there is room for interpretation of the double drag tap (reveille stroke or *Tagwachtstreich*) in bar 5 of the B section and its reversed version in bar 7 of the B part. *Numbers 10 and 11* of →*appendix 1* show the usual form for their interpretation. The structures of the septuplet phrases in *Another Garryowen* are based on the *Siebener Endstreich* (*final strokes of seven*) and *3er Ruf Tagwachtstreichkombination* (*3-stroke roll reveille stroke combination*); the distances between the notes have been changed, however. See also exercises *nos. 20 and 25 of* →*appendix 2*. Be careful in the very last bar—the flam combination is awkward. Make sure the notes are not spread too much; the whole phrase would then sound more like 32nd notes, and the unique character of the flam inside the septuplet would be lost.

See ↓ p. 75

See ↓ p. 83/84.

Another Garryowen

Arranged by Claus Hessler

Dixie

HISTORY AND BACKGROUND

Dixie is most likely one of those tunes where the title itself does not say too much—but everybody knows it once the first two bars are through.

As to the background of the composition, the song was written by Daniel Decatur Emmett (1815–1904) in 1859. Emmett was one of the most important representatives of so-called *minstrel music*, which was very popular around the middle of the 19th century. He served in the U.S. Army, also playing fifes and drums, until his discharge in 1835. *Dixie* was regarded as one of the absolute classics of minstrel music and soon gained tremendous popularity. Emmett's life story was also turned into a film starring Bing Crosby as Emmett (additional music in this movie was composed by Jimmie van Heusen and Johnny Burke). Countless Western movies use *Dixie* as a part of their soundtrack to enhance a more contemporary vibe.

Paramount Pictures: *Dixie* (1943)
DVD available through Simply Media UK

The title *Dixie* is an abbreviated form of the term "I wish I was in Dixie(land)..."—describing the southern states of the U.S. Its origin most likely goes back to the so-called *Mason-Dixon Line*, the demarcation line between Pennsylvania and Maryland, surveyed by Charles Mason and Jeremiah Dixon and separating the union Northern States from the Southern Confederacy. Thus, anywhere south of this line could be called *Dixieland*. Another explanation might be the word *dix*, which was featured on the ten-dollar bill of the Southern States.

Although the piece was well known in both halves of the U.S., it became an unofficial anthem of the Southern Confederacy during the *Civil War* (1861–1865). To this day the song is much more associated with the South, even though Emmett himself was born in the North and strongly condemned the use of his piece as a "war song." Strangely enough, the political leaders of both parties in the *Civil War* used the song for their own purposes, Abraham Lincoln (President of the Union) during his election campaign and Jefferson Davis (President of the Southern States) at his inauguration.

In George Bruce and Daniel Emmett's *The Drummers' and Fifers' Guide*, no stickings are mentioned. Later books give more detailed information although there is still room for individual interpretation. Sanford Moeller's version just adds stickings without changing the music itself. Neither Bruce & Emmett nor Moeller indicate what the crosses and dots above the notes in the C part are meant for.

It seems likely that the crosses indicate a "stick-on-stick" effect with the right stick hitting the left. Apart from that I just provide you with the Bruce & Emmett version along with the stickings from the Moeller book. There is also conflicting information about the length of rolls in the different books—some material shows 13-stroke rolls in measures 5 and 6 of the A part while others display a 15-stroke roll. The triplet-like interpretation of the 7-stroke roll might be technically challenging, and on very authentic and traditional-sounding performances you might want to play beat 1 of the next bar slightly late. Also, make sure that the grace notes of the single drags in the first bar of the B part are adequately spaced so that they sound more or less like 32nd notes.

Dixie – Original Score

Composed by Daniel D. Emmett–Drum Score by George B. Bruce

Stickings based on the version of Sanford Moeller

Track 38: Demo

Track 40: Play-Along

Track 41: Play-Along (slow)

D.C. al Coda

Fine

* This symbol (+) indicates that you should hit the right stick on the left stick, not the drumhead.
  When doing this, the left stick is held above the drumhead and not touching it.

The updated version of *Dixie* has been influenced by reverse syncopation (for reference, check out my double DVD *Drumming Kairos*): Paradiddle sticking has been implemented into the flow of 16th notes to support the melody of the song. You will also find phrases based on the *Siebener Endstreich* (*final stroke of seven*) in which the distances between the notes have been changed (→*Collapsed Rudiments*).

See pp. 79.

Another Dixie

Arranged by Claus Hessler

Track 39: Demo　Track 40: Play-Along　Track 41: Play-Along (slow)

Fine

D.S. con rep. al Fine

𝔜𝔞𝔫𝔨𝔢𝔢 𝔇𝔬𝔬𝔡𝔩𝔢

HISTORY AND BACKGROUND

Along with "Dixie," "Yankee Doodle" is one of the most well-known folk songs associated with North America. Again we'll find some unexpected twists and turns in the history of this tune and how it developed and changed through the years. Inevitably, there is a variety of verses for the *Yankee Doodle*—interestingly enough it was originally a satirical song the British brought to the U.S., making fun of the (later revolting) inhabitants of the colonies in the *New World* that should later become the United States. Just as *Dixie* had been claimed by the Southern Confederacy, *Yankee Doodle* was associated with the Northern States. I assume most of you have at least heard this following verse and chorus of the tune:

"Yankee Doodle went to town
Riding on a pony
Stuck a feather in his hat
And called it macaroni

Yankee Doodle keep it up
Yankee Doodle Dandy
Mind the music and the step
And with the girls be handy."

The term "yankee doodle" is a very uncomplimentary name, describing a person with extremely limited cultural, social, and educational standards, and the lines above make fun of the character. Of course, the Americans added any number of verses that would make fun of the British as well. A free interpretation of the text might be: An American hillbilly takes his workhorse and rides to town. By sticking a feather in his head he thinks he is quite a hot shot. When dancing he has serious difficulties keeping his feet in step, and he does not really know how to behave in female company.

The Spirit of '76 by Archibald MacNeal Willard (1857)

As seen from the British perspective (and not completely without cause) the population in New England around the middle of the 18th century largely consisted of people that mostly did not know much about or appreciate the cultural, artistic, and artisan achievements of Europe and Great Britain, which goes some way in explaining the condescending attitude of the British. It was in fact the British who brought the tune to America during the French and Indian Wars in the second half of the 18th century. They also used the tune during the War of Independence. It did not take long for the Americans to turn the tables. They soon were using the tune to make fun of the British whenever they had lost a military conflict against the supposedly unrefined and badly equipped rebels. It was recorded that the British Army played "Yankee Doodle" on their march to Lexington Green on the morning of April 19, 1775, to mock the Americans. However, after the latter had won the battle, they played the same tune in return to lampoon. Both parties played "Yankee Doodle" at the Battle of Yorktown (1781) as well. There are also reports that claim that allied French troops, fighting with the Americans under General Lafayette, played the tune to further humiliate the defeated British troops.

The famous picture *The Spirit of '76* by Archibald MacNeal Willard conveys the spirit and pride of the revolting colonists in a unique way. For us drummers it is also very interesting to notice the fist-like grip (look at the white-haired drummer in the center of the picture) in the right hand—very much as it is still in use in traditional French and Swiss rudimental drumming, and how it has been described by Samuel Potter. With that in mind, a picture like the one on the previous page is equally as relevant as the drawings by Diebold Schilling the Younger in ancient Swiss chronicles. Now let's turn to the tune itself. Here's a traditional version of "Yankee Doodle":

Yankee Doodle - Original Score

Traditional

By now you will most likely be familiar with most of the phrases used in my updated version. Just two passages might need extra clarification. One of them is a variation with the ending of a final stroke of seven: the two closing 16th notes have been replaced by a combination of 32nd notes and one 16th note, as you can see in the following box:

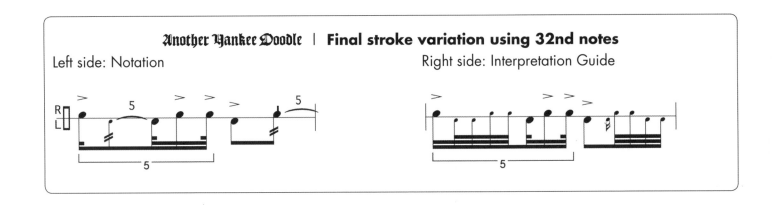

Another Yankee Doodle | **Final stroke variation using 32nd notes**

Left side: Notation

Right side: Interpretation Guide

Field Drum displaying the characteristic eagle depiction used by Sanford Moeller, 20" x 17".

© Cooperman Fife & Drum Co. Inc., Bellows Falls , VT U.S.A.

The other passage is at the very ending of the piece, and uses a rather uncommon method to organize a 13-stroke roll using a polyrhythm of seven over two—which sounds more complicated than it actually feels when playing it. You will be surprised by how smoothly that configuration of strokes can be implemented in the flow of the piece. Although the form of notation using the two grace notes might look strange with the 13-stroke roll, I have still decided to use the symbol by reason of the unusual rhythmic structure and the fact that the roll commences sooner than expected. On beat 2 in the third bar you'll also notice another version of a Swiss final stroke of seven. The very end of the tune includes a flammed coup de charge. This might be somewhat demanding technically, but it is a common feature of Basel drumming.

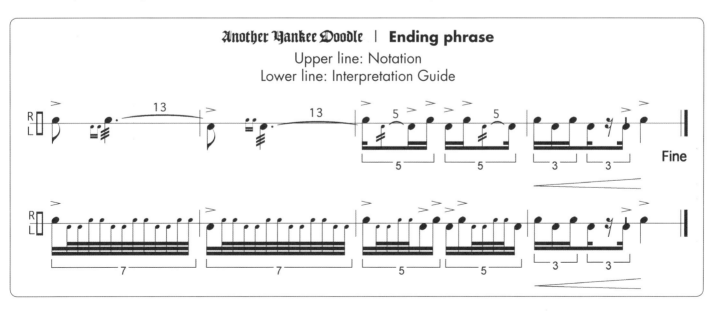

Another Yankee Doodle

Arranged by Claus Hessler

British Grenadiers

HISTORY AND BACKGROUND

"British Grenadiers" is another well-known highlight in the military treasure chest of songs and melodies. As with the previous tunes we have dealt with, there are numerous versions and variations both in terms of the theme and lyrics. According to the research of musicologist Lewis Winstock, the origin of this piece dates back to the late 17th century. Unsurprisingly, the verses speak very highly of the British grenadiers and compare them with the heroes of classical antiquity. Here is one of the many verses that exist:

> "Some talk of Alexander and some of Hercules
> Of Conon and Lysander and some of Meltiadies
> But of all the world's brave heroes there's none that can compare,
> With a tow row row row row
> To the British Grenadiers"

The *tow row row* phrasing most likely seems to relate to the drumming companions of the grenadiers and their military music accompaniment. In his publication *Percussion Instruments and Their History* James Blade suggests a relationship between the terms *tow row row* and the *pou* and *tou* that we have seen in the notation of the *English March*. Personally I think it is more likely to be a more general imitation of the sound of the drums.

Just as with the other tunes in this chapter, the *British Grenadiers* can be looked at as a stand-alone tune without a link to a certain military order. In the *Drum and Flute Duty* of the British Army from 1887, the first four bars of the tune appear as a signal for the *Men's 1st Breakfast and Tea*, however. The *Drum and Flute Duty* also mentions that all signals should commence with a broad, (most likely) accented open flam (or a Swiss *coup de charge*). The notation also shows two 32nd notes played hand-to-hand rather than the regular smaller grace-note indication. The actual piece would then start in the next bar.

Similar to the *Garryowen*, the *British Grenadiers* also made its way into the previously mentioned piece *Arabi* in the songbook of Swiss drummers and fifers. Since folk songs in general were always an important source for the music used in the *Fasnacht*, even a folk song that originated from a different country would still be in keeping with the tradition. As stated before, the first two verses of the *Arabi* represent the theme of the *British Grenadiers* and nine out of ten citizens of Basel will know that melody for sure.

In the version that I describe as original score you'll therefore find a mixture of the chart as found in Bruce & Emmett, and the drum chart as shown by Dr. Fritz Berger in volume 1 of his Swiss marches (*Trommelmärsche Band 1*; see also the list of sources used at the end of this book). The Berger version is made up of typical Swiss ingredients (such as *final strokes of seven* and the *doublé* or *inverted flam tap*) without any notable similarities to the American version. When listening to the CD, you'll also notice that I could not completely resist the temptation to at least have a certain degree of Swiss-like interpretation—tending away from the grid of plain 16th notes. It also has to be mentioned that the theme of the tune itself has been subject to several changes throughout the years so it is not possible to present the "one and only" original version of the piece.

Track 46: Demo
Track 48: Play-Along
Track 49: Play-Along (slow)

British Grenadiers – Original Score

Traditional

Parts A and B based on: The Drummers' & Fifers' Guide (Bruce & Emmett)

Parts C and D based on: Trommelmärsche Band 1 (Dr. Fritz Berger) —Verses 1 & 2 of the "Arabi"

As with "Yankee Doodle," the updated version uses a modified framework of Swiss final strokes with 32nd notes added to the traditional structures. It also includes a number of typical ingredients from the school of Basel drumming: first the *coup de charge*, which is featured at the very beginning of the tune as well as in the first endings of the A and C parts, and then the *doublé* (or *inverted flam tap*) and the *single drag tap* (or *Rigodon*). The triple grace notes (or 4-stroke ruffs) in the C and D parts might turn out to be challenging. But you should note that these structures are based simply on *double drag taps* (or *Tagwachtstreich*), except that the drags have been replaced by 4-stroke ruffs. Again, I strongly recommend practicing the collection of exercises based on quintuplets at the end of this book. For example, *exercise no. 10* of →*appendix 2* would be relevant for the 7-stroke rolls in this piece.

See p. 81.

Another Grenadier

Arranged by Claus Hessler

Inside the shell of a William Kilbourn field drum, built 1864

© Cooperman Fife & Drum Co. Inc., Bellows Falls, VT U.S.A.

CHAPTER 4 | RUDIMENTS ON DRUMSET: DIFFERENT PROSPECTS

Applying rudiments on the drumset has always been an important subject for many drummers—using them as a source for inspiration and different ways of musical expression. In my publications *Drumming Kairos* (double DVD, including a 120-page PDF booklet) and *Open-Handed Playing Vol. 2: A Step Beyond*, you'll find a few different approaches. (*Note*: Whether you use these ideas in the "open-handed" mode or with hands crossed is not necessarily the issue. You might just have a few more options in the open-handed mode as opposed to playing with hands crossed. The concepts themselves are the decisive factor.) I'm sure you'll find some very realistic and useful tips in these books that will definitely enrich your playing and drumming vocabulary and offer some different and unusual approaches.

Here's a list of strategies when using rudiments on the drumset:

• Experiment with different rhythmic layers

Talking straight: Play a flam accent using a shuffled rhythm, a single flammed mill using triplets, a Swiss army triplet using 16th notes, a 5-stroke roll using quintuplets, etc.

• Experiment with the distances between the strokes

This is the strategy behind *collapsed rudiments*. Originally a playground of the late great Jim Chapin, this is all about changing the distances between the notes but staying with the same sticking of a pattern. The double DVD *Drumming Kairos* also offers an introduction to this subject and includes an educational poster created in collaboration with Dom Famularo explaining the topic further, and showing relationships between different rudiments that share the same sticking.

• Experiment with the exact configuration of notes on flams

The strokes involved in a flam could also be executed as so-called *flat flams*, a term used by Joe Morello. Another option would be to use a rhythmically defined position for the strokes (e.g., 32nd notes).

• Experiment with various dynamics/accents

At first, try to stay with the original accents as described in the rudimental pattern itself. Then experiment with different positions for accents, and find out if that helps with your musical expression.

• Experiment with different orchestration around the drums

Spread the pattern around the drums, and don't limit yourself to assigning only one sound to one limb at a time. Also think about including the feet and replacing notes correspondingly.

• Experiment with combinations of rudiments of similar structure

When combining several rudiments it is interesting to first think about which ones have a similar genetic blueprint. To go from flam, to flam tap, to Swiss army triplet, to single flammed mill, you just need to add one extra stroke at each stage, for instance. The same applies for the flam, inverted flam tap, flam accent, and pataflafla. *Open-Handed Playing Vol. 2: A Step Beyond* has a variety of organized and systematic exercises that make use of these relationships. There are, of course, other relationships between rudiments, but that goes beyond the scope of this chapter and would be another story to tell.

In some cases it is also possible to transfer certain passages from snare to drumset with little or no additional conceptual effort, bringing quite surprising results. Here are some excerpts from "Another Grenadier" that have been orchestrated between hi-hat, snare drum, and bass drum. The upper line shows the original snare part as shown with the piece, while the lower line is the adaptation for drumset. The result is perhaps unusual but very intriguing:

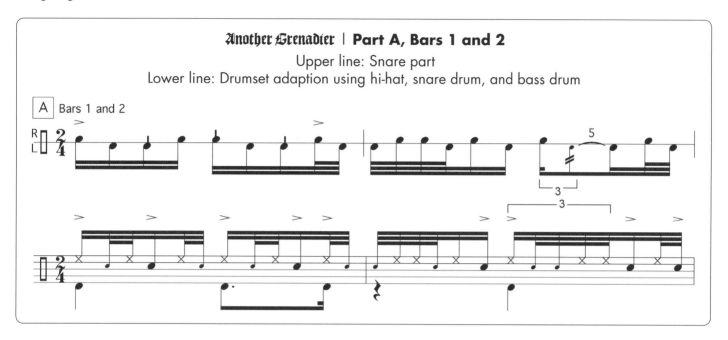

Another Grenadier | Part A, Bars 1 and 2
Upper line: Snare part
Lower line: Drumset adaption using hi-hat, snare drum, and bass drum

The transfer to drumset uses very few principles: The strokes of the flam in the first bar have been moved apart, and extra accents have been added, while the rest pretty much remains unchanged. The positioning of bass drum notes does not follow any particular rules. In case you are wondering, I would prefer to play these examples open-handed—which also implies that you have to use the reversed sticking of the original snare part. You can do that, too, if you like, but you don't have to. In the long run it will turn out to be an advantage if you are able to perform certain passages with either hand leading.

For the next example I randomly added more dynamics, and the flam in the second bar has become a "flat flam," meaning it is to be played with both hands in unison. The rest remains unchanged.

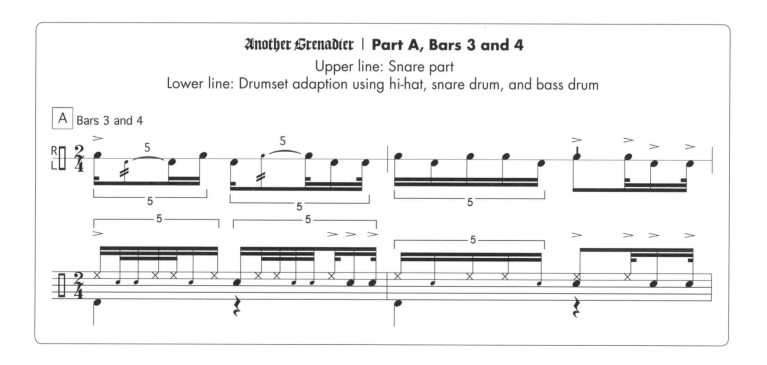

Another Grenadier | Part A, Bars 3 and 4
Upper line: Snare part
Lower line: Drumset adaption using hi-hat, snare drum, and bass drum

Again there are very few substantial changes in the next box. The flam on beat 1 of the first bar has been left out. As I have again put the notes of the other flams on a 32nd-note grid, the grace note of the flam on beat 1 in the second bar appears to show up at the very end of the first measure:

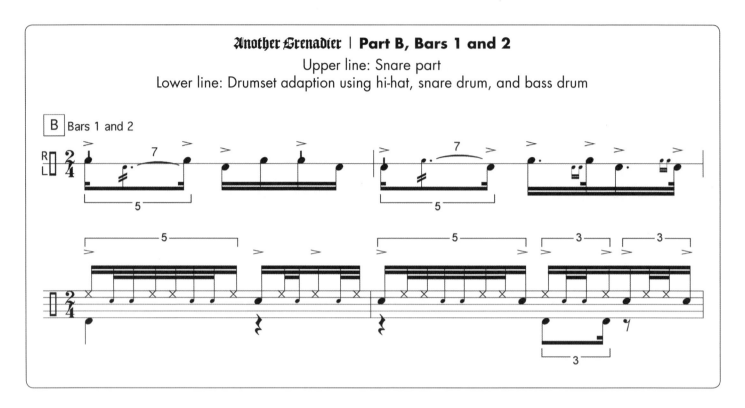

The next example follows the same strategies; certain challenges might be connected with the bass drum notes embedded in the flow of the quintuplet in the first bar. Make sure that the hands and feet play exactly together:

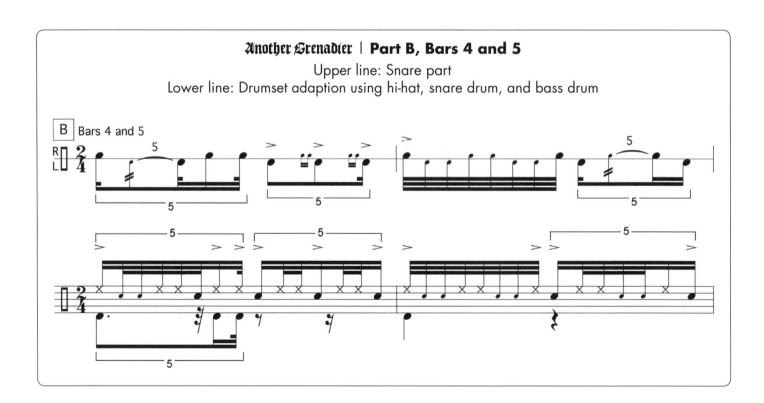

The following sequence features a slight variation with regard to orchestration around the drumset. This time, the snare part is played between two different hi-hats on both sides of the kit. As an option you may also use a combination of ride cymbals and hi-hat. Patterns like these are great to spice up certain grooves and add some extra, unexpected excitement. Again you should watch out for possible challenges with the bass drum strokes on the quintuplet grid.

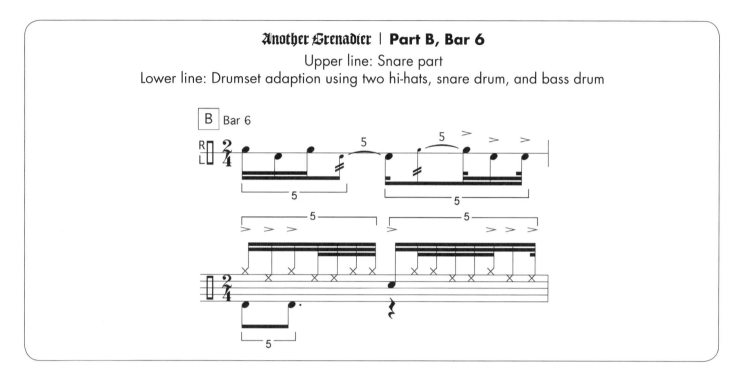

Another Grenadier | Part B, Bar 6

Upper line: Snare part
Lower line: Drumset adaption using two hi-hats, snare drum, and bass drum

The next two measures taken from part C of the piece feature additional accents; in the second bar I brought in an open hi-hat sound for the embellishment on beat 2. The flammed 5-stroke roll has been orchestrated using the concept of flat flams again:

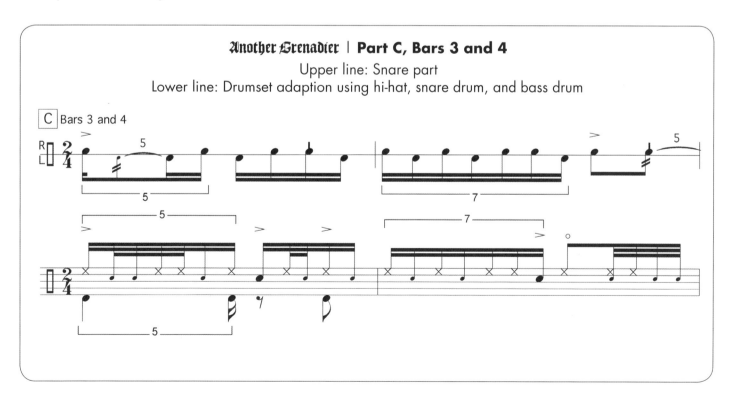

Another Grenadier | Part C, Bars 3 and 4

Upper line: Snare part
Lower line: Drumset adaption using hi-hat, snare drum, and bass drum

The different approaches used so far have also been incorporated into the last two examples. It goes without saying that you do not have to use the complete phrase but may also just embed parts of all these patterns into your own phrases and grooves whenever you feel the need:

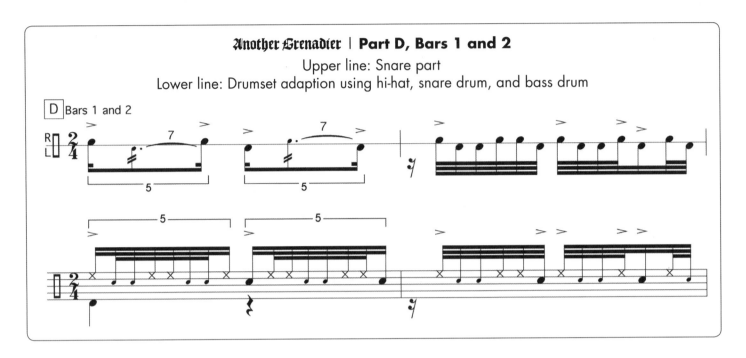

Another Grenadier | Part D, Bars 1 and 2

Upper line: Snare part
Lower line: Drumset adaption using hi-hat, snare drum, and bass drum

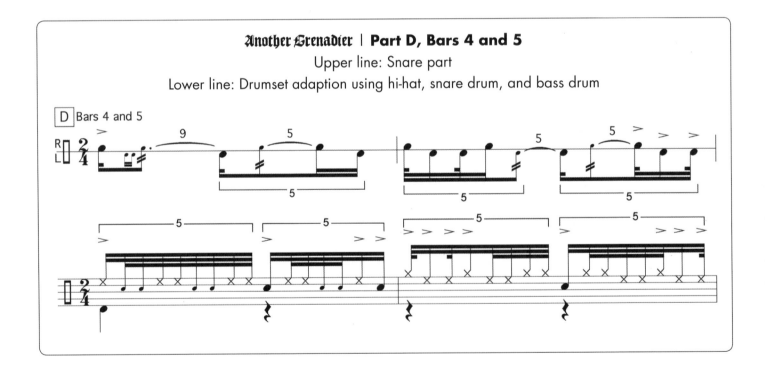

Another Grenadier | Part D, Bars 4 and 5

Upper line: Snare part
Lower line: Drumset adaption using hi-hat, snare drum, and bass drum

See pp. 79. *One more final hint:* Using these strategies as shown with the previous examples and orchestrating the patterns between hi-hat and snare from → *appendix 2* will generate a wealth of very interesting phrases that will undoubtedly enrich your drumming vocabulary. Check it out and be surprised!

APPENDIX 1
RUDIMENTS AND THEIR NAMES IN DIFFERENT AREAS AND ERAS

The following chart shows an overview of similar or identical phrases and their corresponding denotation. This list does not claim to be complete; I focused on patterns...

- appearing in different rudimental schools of drumming or under different names
- which are often the subject of mistaken identity, and
- are of a certain relevance regarding the pieces in this book.

The more you become acquainted with the history of drumming and work your way into the material, the more you come across terms and descriptions that are hardly found any more these days. Some of them are quite easy to reconstruct (e.g., faint stroke or faint flam; with "faint" meaning weak or soft), while some of them turn out to be hard to trace back to their original meaning (as with the "poing stroke," for instance). In order not to endanger the clarity of the chart I also reduced the amount of background details for certain rudiments. There are two possible reasons why the name of a rudiment might not appear in one of the columns (U.S.: Traditional, U.S.: Contemporary, France, and Switzerland):

First, the corresponding pattern simply does not exist in that school of drumming;

Second, the phrase does exist but there is possibly no extra term for it. Sometimes it just happens that certain stickings appear within a piece, but there is not always a real name for them.

	U.S.—Traditional	U.S.—Contemporary	France	Switzerland
1		Single-stroke roll	Baton Rond; Coup Simple	Zitterstreich
	Note: Comes before no. 1 in the first official list of rudiments.			
2	Long roll	Open roll	Baton Rompu	Mama Papa
	Note: Many ancient sources show this rudiment starting with the left hand. Old U.S. sources and drum manuals usually start with the "long roll," hardly ever with the "single-stroke roll."			
3	Close flam; Flam	Flam	Fla	Schleppstreich
	Note: "Close flam" appears with Samuel Potter's *The Art of Beating the Drum*. The abbreviated shorthand for the flam using the small line inside the note head is found commonly in Swiss notation.			

	U.S.—Traditional	U.S.—Contemporary	France	Switzerland
4	Hard flam; Open flam			Coup de Charge; (*Charge stroke*)
	Note: "Open flam" appears with Samuel Potter's *The Art of Beating the Drum.* "Hard flam" is a term used by Charles Ashworth *A New, Useful and Complete System of Drum Beating.* The notation on the right side appears commonly in Switzerland.			
5			Coup de Charge; Part of coup de coulé	
	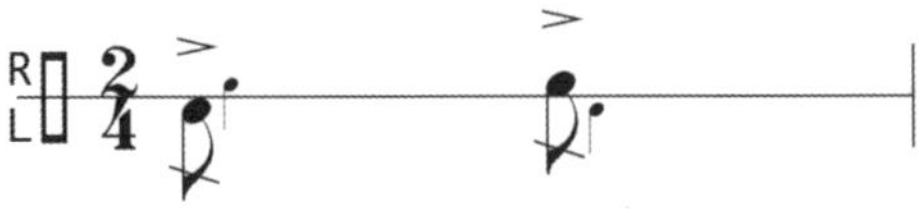 Note: This phrase is exclusively connected with the French drumming tradition. The grace note is accented while the main note is performed rather softly.			
6	Stroke and flam	Flam tap	Batard	
7	Flam and stroke; English stroke; Tap flam	Inverted flam tap	Coup Anglais	Doublé
	 Note: In Switzerland and France this phrase normally appears using a 16th-note structure (see middle example) though not always with the accents as shown here; dynamics may vary. The interpretation can tend towards quintuplet phrasing as seen in the example on the right.			
8	Ruffe; Ruff; Half drag	Drag	Ra de Trois	3er Ruf (*literally: a "call" of 3*)
	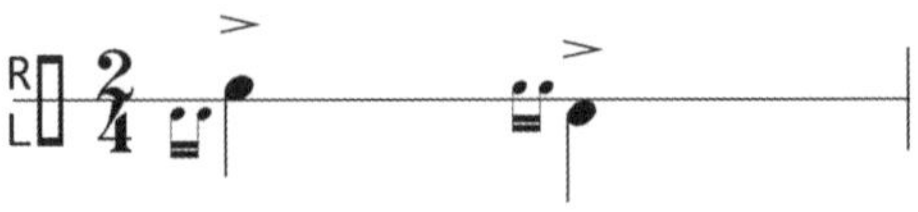 Note: "Ruffe" and "Ruff" are very likely derived from the German word "Ruf" (literally meaning "call"; used to describe a "roll"). In the first list of rudiments by the NARD this pattern was still called a "ruff," not a "drag." The word "drag" might have its origin in the process of dragging the stick more or less across the drumhead to produce two notes. The term "half drag" can be found in Charles Ashworth's writing.			
9	Single drag	Single drag tap	Rigodon	Rigodon-Streich

	U.S.—Traditional	**U.S.—Contemporary**	**France**	**Switzerland**
9	Single drag	Single drag tap	Rigodon	Rigodon-Streich
10	Double drag	Double-drag tap	Coup de la Diane	Einfacher Tagwachtstreich (*Single reveille stroke*)
	Note: The left and middle bars are just two different versions of notation for the same rudiment. The third measure describes the actual rhythmic interpretation, giving the double strokes a concrete place and time within the phrase. The pattern may also be regarded as a shifted version of *no. 27* in →*appendix 1.*			
11				Umgekehrter, einfacher Tagwachtstreich (*Reversed single reveille stroke*)
	Note: Although very common in Swiss drumming, in the U.S. catalog of rudiments there is no such thing as a reversed double drag tap. The bar on the left is a common form of notation while the right bar refers to the actual interpretation. Dynamics may vary.			
12	Quick Scotch	Lesson 25	Raté Sauté de Trois	
	Note: This pattern appears in the piece Quick Scotch (also contained in the U.S. Camp Duty) and was even called that in the first list of rudiments. As the piece (and the pattern) was the last in the process of the reveille, it was placed at no. 25 on the list of rudiments, and the name "lesson 25" became more frequent. Together with the "single-stroke roll" (which had no number), we finally had 26 rudiments.			
13	Double ratamacue	Double ratamacue		Triplierter, einfacher Tagwachtstreich (*Tripled single reveille stroke*)
	Note: Another of the "old" rudiments with a description/name imitating the sound of the phrase. In Swiss drumming this was mostly used with reveilles to wake up troops. Closely related to the double drag tap (or single reveille stroke).			

↓ See p. 78.

	U.S.—Traditional	U.S.—Contemporary	France	Switzerland
14	Single paradidle	Single paradiddle	Moulin	Mühle; (Mill, mill stroke)

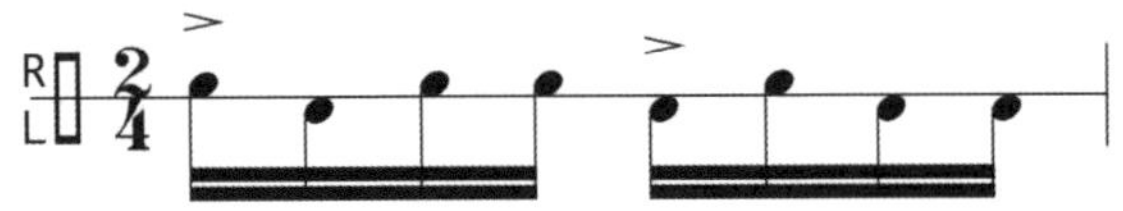

Note: The paradiddle is also known as "Mühlestreich" (German: literally, "mill stroke") or "Moulin" (French for "mill stroke") both in its standard form and using inverted sticking. In Germany, the "Mühle" still refers to alternating double strokes with increasing/decreasing speed. This difference might have resulted from an incorrect copy of a German drum duty around 1800.

15	Windmill	Single flammed mill		Schleppmühle (Flammed mill)

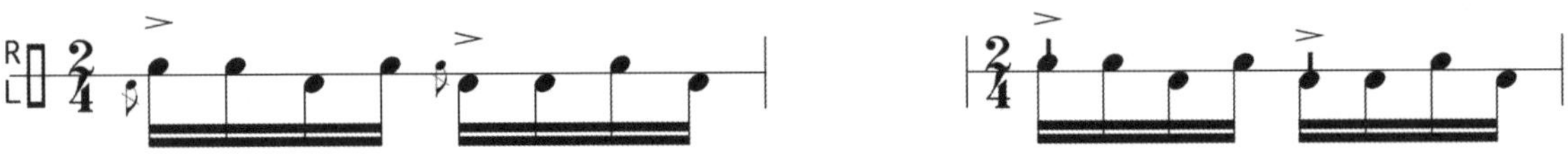

Note: The explanations given with no. 14 of this list can also be applied to the term "single flammed mill." It is a direct translation of the Swiss description of the pattern. The measure on the right again uses the abbreviated form of notation for the flam.

16			Patatrata	3er Ruf Mühle (3-stroke roll mill)

Note: In Swiss notation additional ornaments (e.g., flams, drags, or ruffs) are often placed in different corners of the basic paradiddle pattern to help make execution easier and more comfortable. The one shown here is much easier to perform (comparable to the difference between the flamadiddle and the single flammed mill). The French term relates to the imitation of sound as shown with the example on the right.

17	Double paradidle	Double paradiddle	Coup Volant	

18	Mother; 5-roll	5-stroke roll	Ra de Cinq	5er Ruf; (literally: a "call" of 5)

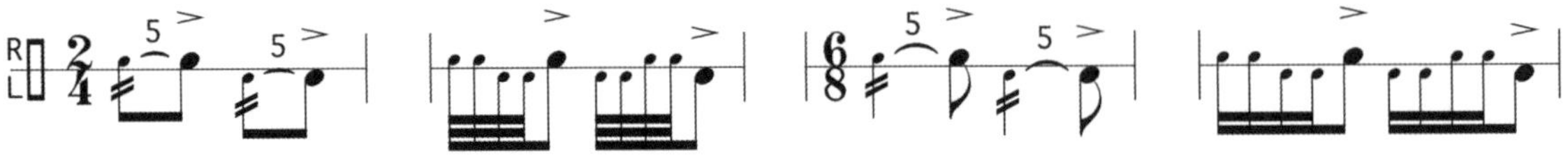

Note: Note: "Mother" was a widespread term in traditional sources in English (Charles Ashworth, Samuel Potter); "5-roll" is a term used in Col. H. C. Hart's New and Improved Instructor for the Drum. The pattern appears in various rhythmic shapes, ranging from 32nd notes to triplets, and even to quintuplets in the French tradition. In old sources the phrase mostly starts with the left hand, while the fifth note is an accent.

	U.S.—Traditional	**U.S.—Contemporary**	**France**	**Switzerland**
19		Flammed 5-stroke roll		5er Schleppruf (*Flammed 5-stroke roll*)

Note: Rolls commencing with a flam appear frequently in Swiss rudimental drumming. The pattern here shows a change of the leading hand.

20	7-roll; 7-stroke roll	7-stroke roll	Ra de Sept	7er Ruf (*a "call" of 7*)

Note: The 7-stroke roll also appears in different rhythmic shapes, using triplets or a 16th-note/32nd-note subdivision (Charley Wilcoxon indicated the difference between the two using an additional "drag" sign (which is NOT an additional drag before the roll but really a part of the roll itself).

21	9-roll; 9-stroke roll	9-stroke roll	Ra de Neuf	9er Ruf (*a "call" of 9*)

Note: In this book, the 9-stroke roll often appears using quintuplet subdivision (see bars 3 and 4). The additional "drag" sign is meant to indicate exactly that (similar to the Wilcoxon strategy with 7-stroke rolls). It would also be possible to commence the 9-stroke roll with a flam and make it a "flamed" version (*see no. 19* of this list).

22		Swiss army triplet		Schweizer Ordonnanztriole

Note: In the Swiss drumming tradition, this pattern was meant to be a simplified version of the flam accent since it does not change hands. In general, Swiss "ordinance drumming" usually has fewer ornaments and avoids the trickier patterns that are used in Basel drumming.

23		Flam accent	Patafla	Schlepptriole (*Flammed triplet*)

	U.S.—Traditional	U.S.—Contemporary	France	Switzerland
24		Pataflafla	Pataflafla	Bataflafla-Streich

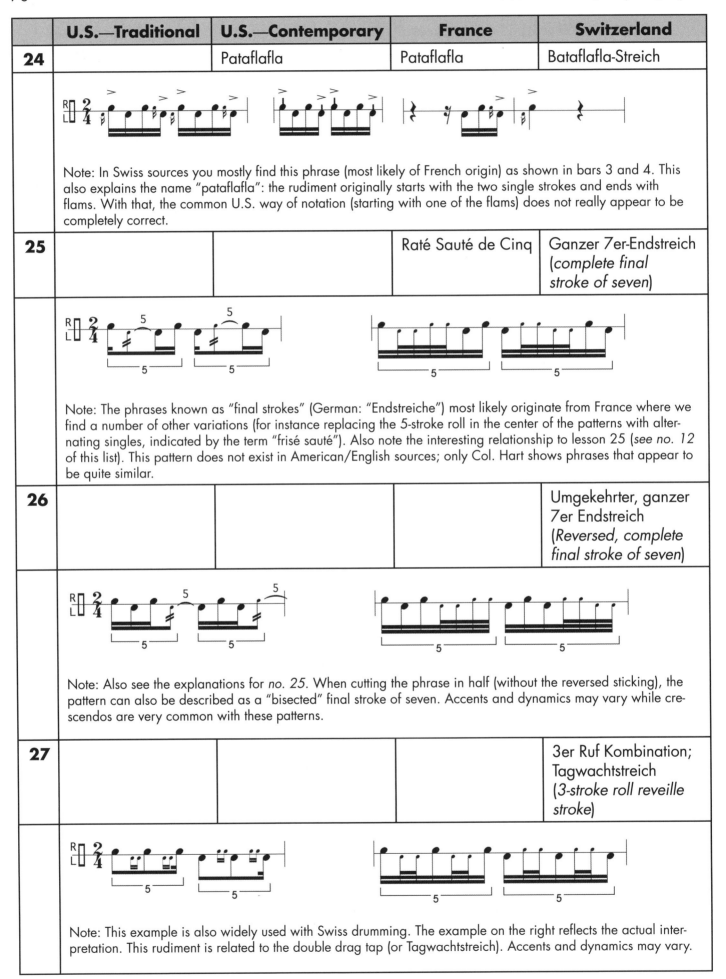

Note: In Swiss sources you mostly find this phrase (most likely of French origin) as shown in bars 3 and 4. This also explains the name "pataflafla": the rudiment originally starts with the two single strokes and ends with flams. With that, the common U.S. way of notation (starting with one of the flams) does not really appear to be completely correct.

25			Raté Sauté de Cinq	Ganzer 7er-Endstreich (*complete final stroke of seven*)

Note: The phrases known as "final strokes" (German: "Endstreiche") most likely originate from France where we find a number of other variations (for instance replacing the 5-stroke roll in the center of the patterns with alternating singles, indicated by the term "frisé sauté"). Also note the interesting relationship to lesson 25 (*see no. 12* of this list). This pattern does not exist in American/English sources; only Col. Hart shows phrases that appear to be quite similar.

26				Umgekehrter, ganzer 7er Endstreich (*Reversed, complete final stroke of seven*)

Note: Also see the explanations for *no. 25*. When cutting the phrase in half (without the reversed sticking), the pattern can also be described as a "bisected" final stroke of seven. Accents and dynamics may vary while crescendos are very common with these patterns.

27				3er Ruf Kombination; Tagwachtstreich (*3-stroke roll reveille stroke*)

Note: This example is also widely used with Swiss drumming. The example on the right reflects the actual interpretation. This rudiment is related to the double drag tap (or Tagwachtstreich). Accents and dynamics may vary.

APPENDIX 2
RUDIMENTS | QUINTUPLETS | COLLAPSED & UNCOLLAPSED RUDIMENTS

Especially in my own, updated versions of the pieces in this book, I frequently use patterns based on quintuplets along with the system of so-called *collapsed rudiments*, in which the distances between the strokes are changed without changing the sticking itself. The following collection of exercises will give you some more material to work on and also allow some insight into how I came up with certain phrases. Let me explain the system of how the exercises are constructed using the example below:

- The basis of unaccented, alternating single strokes is the starting point.

- The group of exercises appearing in a pair of two lines share the same basic structure. In many cases not even the sticking changes, but only the rhythmic order of strokes.

- Bar 1 of *exercise 1* is a possible accent variation.

- The next bar features a double stroke at the position where the accent was before. Don't worry about trying to accent the second note of the double stroke as well—this note should more or less just be a side-effect of the first accented stroke.

- The third bar represents an *uncollapsed* variation: All notes of the pattern should be the same distance to each other. The accents stay within the pattern—but appear in a different rhythmic spot.

- The next bar features an accented flam in the position where the accent was (compare *ex. 1* of *no. 1*).

- The first bar in the second line doubles all the unaccented notes.

- The next bar is again an *uncollapsed* version: all notes are spaced out equally, while the accent is still in play.

- In the the next bar, all the positions of the quintuplet are doubled, including the accent.

- The last bar features a *collapsed* version. By changing the distances between the notes you produce a continuous flow of flammed notes. *Important*: There has to be a clear difference between the accented and unaccented flams (see also the corresponding exercises in the chapter *Reverse Syncopation* in *Drumming Kairos*).

- Make your choice of a combination of any bars (e.g., *Basis* and *no. 1 of ex. 1*), and stay with that combination for a certain amount of time (e.g., one minute), then continue (e.g., *no. 1 of ex. 1* and *no. 2 of ex. 1*), and so forth. Use a metronome, and tap the quarter notes with your foot!

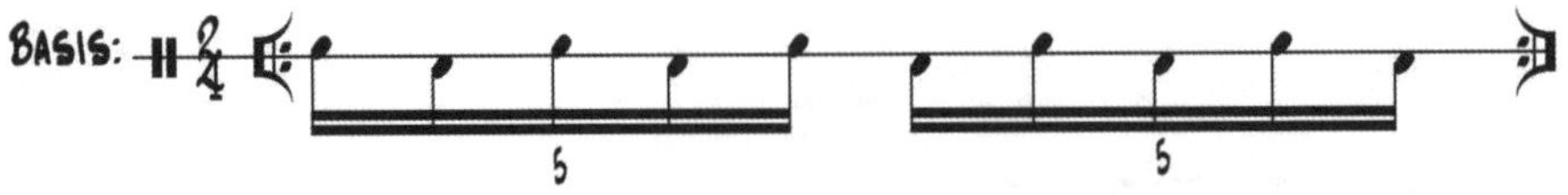

1

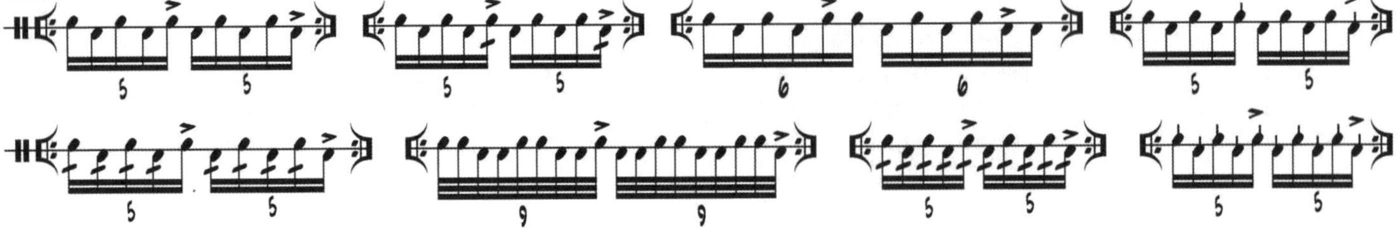

2

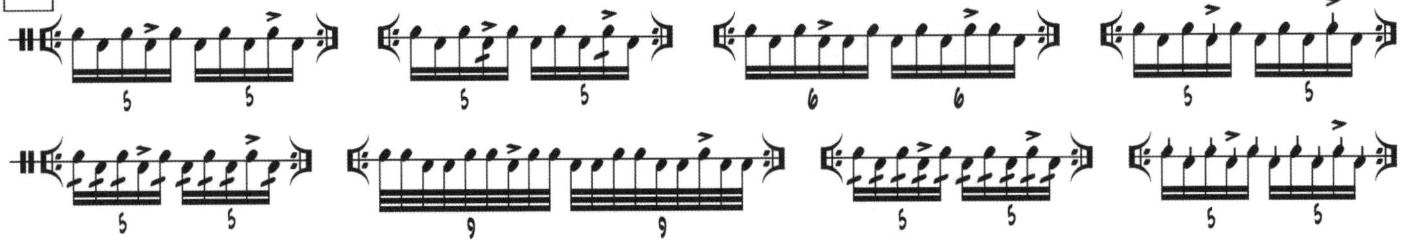

3

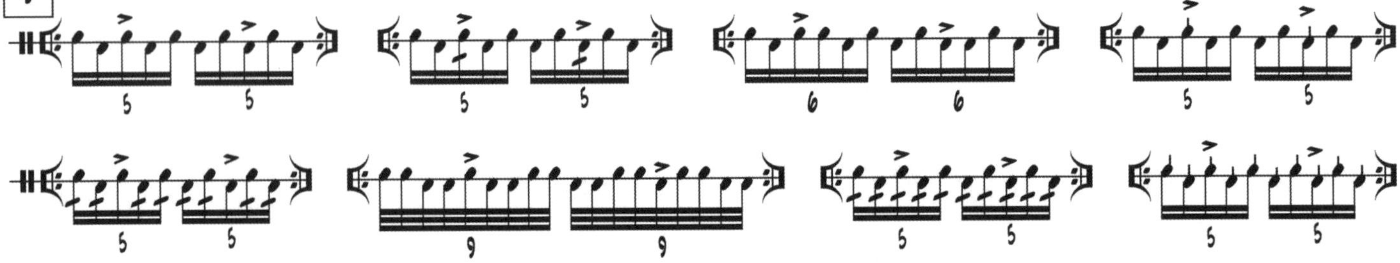

4

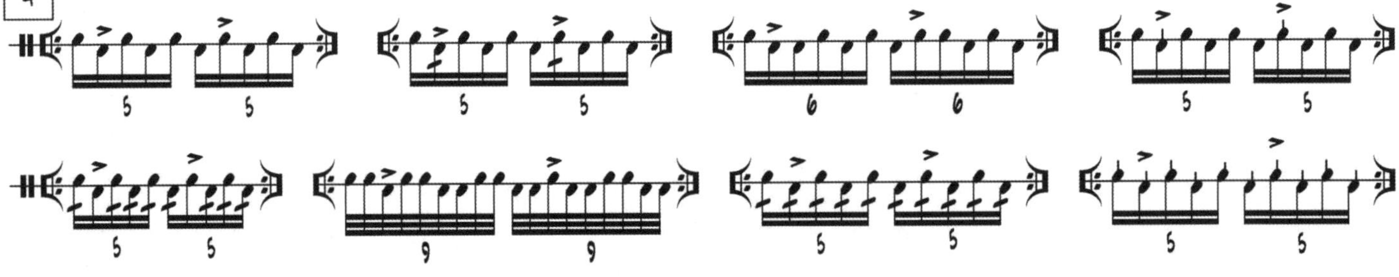

5

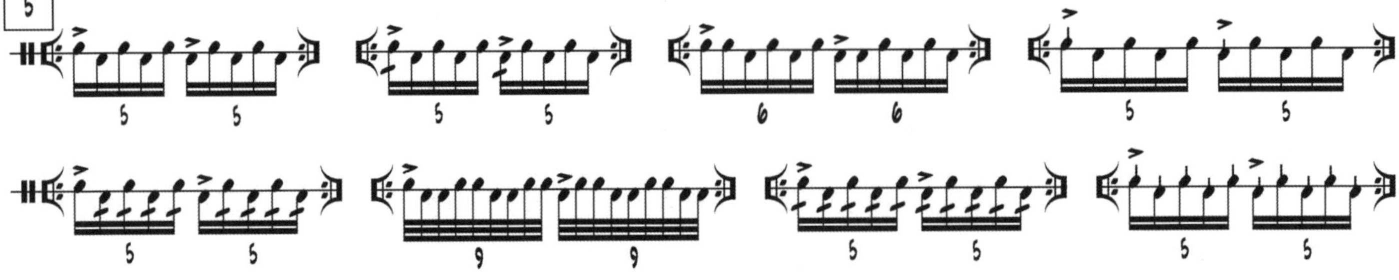

6

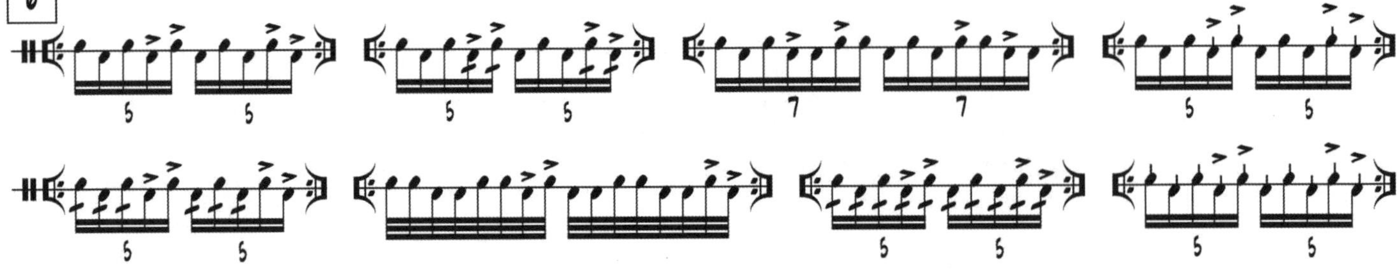

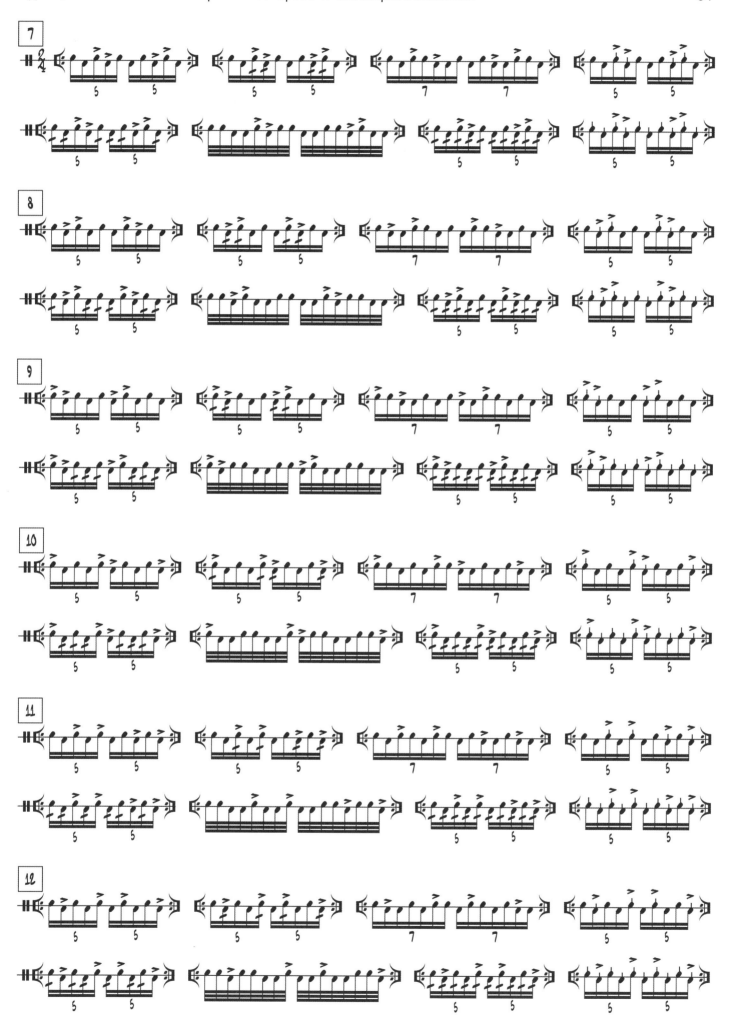

13

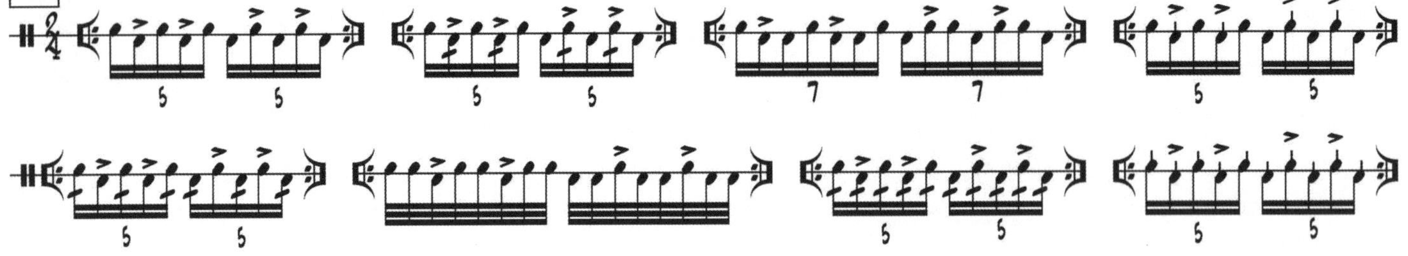

14

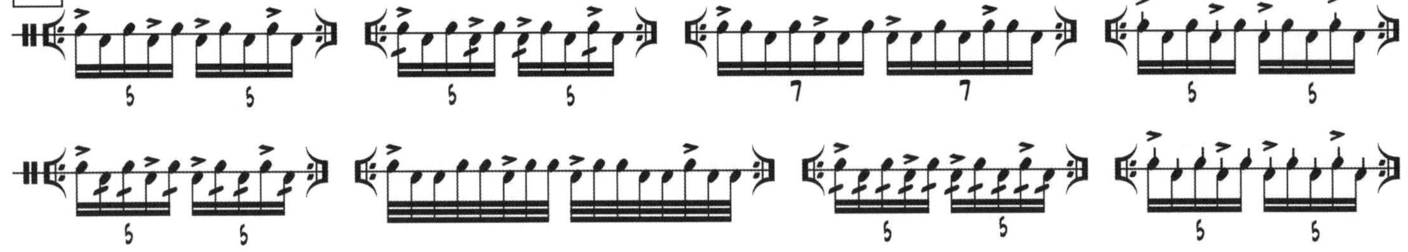

15

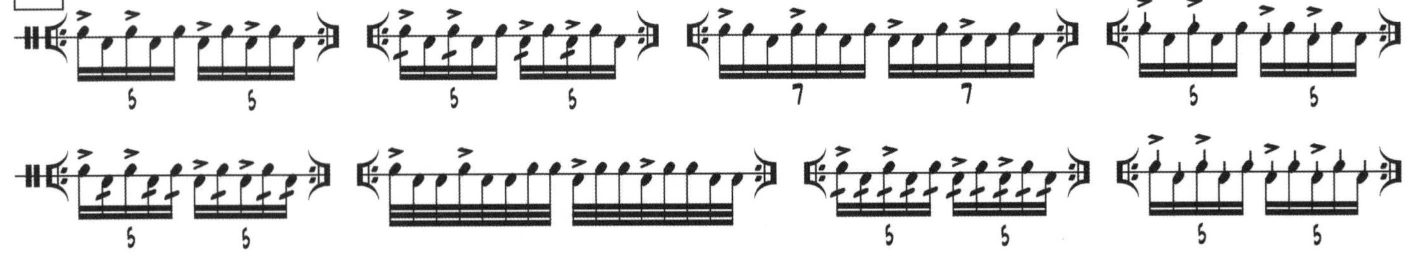

16

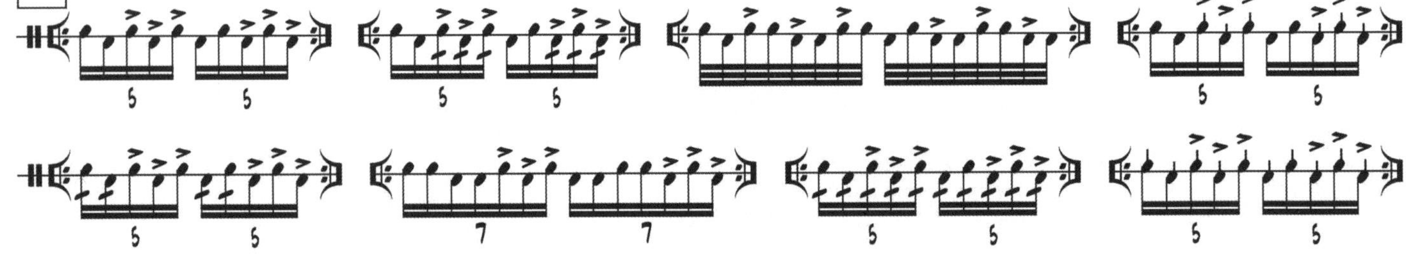

17

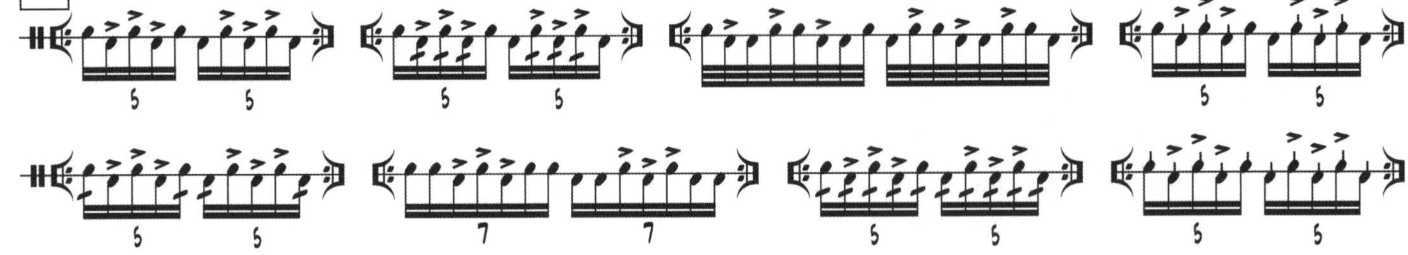

18

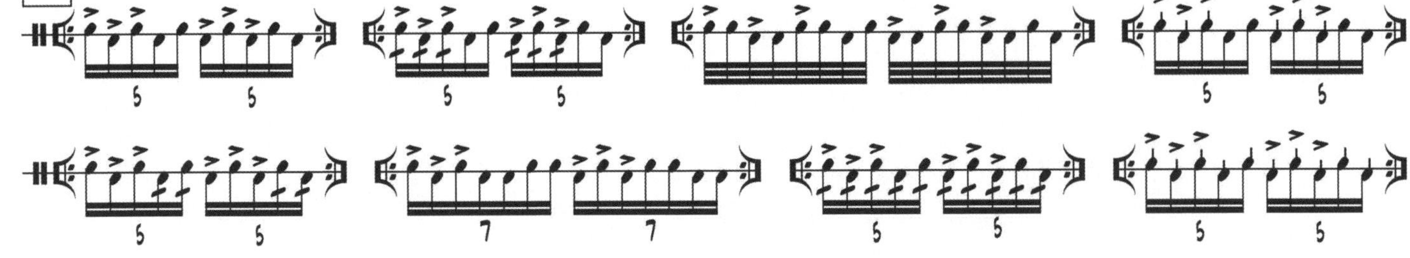

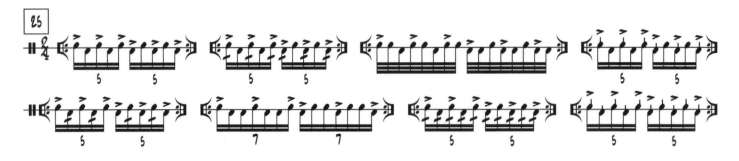

APPENDIX 3:
SOURCES AND MATERIALS USED

The following sources were referred to in the writing of this book (in chronological order of publishing date):

Title	Written by	Published by
Orchésographie	Thoinot Arbeau	First published 1589 Reprint: Dover Publications Inc., Mineola, New York
Il Torneo	Bonaventura Pistofilo	Presso Clemente Ferrone, 1627
Warlike Directions: Or The Souldiers Practice: Set Forth for the Benefit of All Such as Are, Or Will be Scholars of Martiall Discipline. But Especially for All Such Officers as are Not Yet Setled, Or Rightly Grounded in the Arte of Warre	Thomas Fisher	Thomas Harper, London, 1644
General History of the Science and Practice of Music in Five Volumes	Sir John Hawkins	T. Payne & Son, London, 1776
Kurze Anweisung, das Trommel-Spielen auf die leichteste Art zu erlernen. Mit Anmerkungen eines Tonkünstlers	Anonymous	Printed by Georg Ludwig Winters Witwe, Berlin, 1777
Baron von Steuben's Revolutionary War Drill Manual	Frederick William Baron von Steuben	First published 1794	Reprint: Dover Publications Inc., New York
Über das Trommelschlagen	Anonymous	Released in the book store of Commerzienrath Maßdorff, 1801
The Irish Melodies	Thomas Moore	James and William Power Publishers, Dublin, 1808–1834
Over Het Tromslaan	Anonymous	J.S. Van Esveldt-Holtrop, Koninklijk' Boekhandelaar, 1809
A New, Useful and Complete System of Drum Beating	Charles Ashworth	Washington D.C., 1812
The Art of Beating the Drum	Samuel Potter	Published by Henry Potter, UK, 1815	Reprint available at http://www.beafifer.com
The Drummers Assistant or the Art of Drumming Made Easy	Levi Lovering	Printed for the Author by J. G. Klemm, Philadelphia, 1818
The Army Drum and Fife Book	Keach, Burditt, and Cassidy	Published by Oliver Ditson and Co., Boston, 1861
New & Improved Instructor for the Drum	Col. H. C. Hart	Published by the Author, New York, 1862
The Drummers' and Fifers' Guide	George B. Bruce and Daniel D. Emmett	Published by Wm. A. Pond & Co., New York, 1865
Strube's Drum and Fife Instructor	Gardiner A. Strube	Gardiner A. Strube, 1869
Méthode de Tambour et Caisse Claire d'Orchestre	Robert Tourte	Editions Salabert, Paris, 1946

Title	Written by	Published by
The Art of Drumming	J. Burns Moore	Published by W. F. L. Drum Co., Chicago, 1954
The Art of Snare Drumming	Sanford Moeller	Ludwig Music Publishing, Cleveland, Ohio, 1956
Percussion Instruments and Their History	James Blades	Faber & Faber Ltd., London, 1970
Songs & Music of the Redcoats: A History of the War Music of the British Army 1642–1902	Lewis Winstock	Stackpole Books, Harrisburg, 1970
Basler Trommelmärsche Band 1–3	Dr. Fritz Berger	Hug & Co. Musikverlag, Zürich, 1972
Musick of the Fife & Drums, Vol. II: Slow Marches	John C. Moon	The Colonial Williamsburg Foundation, 1977
Le Tambour d'Ordonnance Vol. I–IV	Robert Goute	Editions Robert Martin, Charnay-les-Macon, 1982
Trommeln und Pfeifen in Basel	Georg Duthaler	Christoph Merian Verlag, Basel, 1985
The Drum	Hugh Barty-King	The Royal Tournament, Horse Guards, Whitehall, London, 1988
Encyclopedia of Percussion	Edited by John H. Beck	Routledge, New York, 2007
Connecticut's Fife and Drum Tradition	James Clark	Wesleyan University Press, Middletown, 2011

DRUMMING KAIROS
Get Ready for the Sweet Spot

Playing the drums is a continuous chain of "magic moments." Whenever the moment seems right, there is a perfect time for everything. Being aware of those "sweet spots" is one thing, but being able to take action at exactly the right moment is the common thread that great drummers of all styles share. This dual-language 2-DVD set (with a PDF booklet and poster) will increase your awareness of the sweet spot and give you the tools to bring your musical imagination into the real world. (Languages: English/German). More than 5 hours video material. NTSC version!

2 DVDs   ISBN: 978-3-943638-53-0

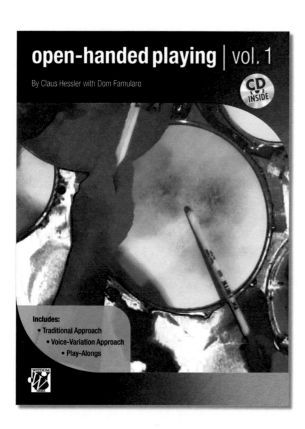

This groundbreaking step-by-step approach for drummers of all styles provides you to learn and apply the concept of open-handed playing on the modern drumset. Based on concepts developed by teaching great Jim Chapin and fusion legend Billy

OPEN-HANDED PLAYING | VOLUME 1
Book & CD   ISBN: 978-0-7390-5415-4

Cobham, Open-Handed Playing not only outlines all the benefits of avoiding the crossing of hands when playing the drumset, but provides an incredibly detailed, complete, and approachable method for learning this technique.

OPEN-HANDED PLAYING | VOLUME 2
A Step Beyond
Book & CD   ISBN: 978-0-7390-8473-1

DAILY DRUMSET WORKOUT
A Day-to-Day Guide to Better Drumming

A comprehensive 224-page publication by the open-handed playing specialist,
Claus Hessler! Here you can find everything a contemporary drummer needs to be able to play
today. Claus teaches you new rhythmic skills that facilitate greater security and musical freedom.
Whether you play rock, pop, funk, Latin, jazz, Afro-Cuban, or second-line music, the high-quality
MP3 CD enables you to practice every exercise in every style in three different tempos.

Book & mp3-CD | 224 pages | ISBN: 978-3-943638-00-4